HAMLYN ALL COLOUR
TEATIME
FAVOURITES

HAMLYN ALL COLOUR
TEATIME
FAVOURITES

HAMLYN

Front cover shows, left to right:
Crunchy cheesecake tart (recipe 229), Aladinn's cave gâteau (recipe 157),
Mini pizzas (recipe 49).

Back cover shows, clockwise from top left:
Raspberry vol-au-vents (recipe 113), Bath buns (recipe 21), Florentines (recipe 197),
Granary bread (recipe 1), Angel cake (recipe 69).

First published in Great Britain l994 by Hamlyn
an imprint of Reed Consumer Books Limited
Michelin House, 81 Fulham Road, London SW3 6RB
and Auckland, Melbourne, Singapore and Toronto.

Copyright © l994 Reed International Books Limited

Line drawings by Graham Bingham
Photographs from Reed Consumer Books Picture Library

ISBN 0 600 58272 8

Recipes in this book were first published under other
Reed Consumer Books imprints.

Produced by Mandarin Offset
Printed and bound in Hong Kong

OTHER TITLES IN THIS SERIES INCLUDE

Hamlyn All Colour Cookbook
Hamlyn New All Colour Cookbook
Hamlyn All Colour Vegetarian Cookbook
Hamlyn New All Colour Vegetarian Cookbook
Hamlyn All Colour Casseroles Cookbook
Hamlyn All Colour Barbecues Cookbook
Hamlyn All Colour Meals in Minutes
Hamlyn All Colour Italian Cookbook
Hamlyn All Colour Salads
Hamlyn All Colour Chinese Cookbook
Hamlyn All Colour Indian Cookbook
Hamlyn All Colour Million Menus Cookbook

CONTENTS

INTRODUCTION

Hamlyn All Colour Teatime Favourites is an invaluable collection of recipes for cakes, biscuits, teabreads, gâteaux, small cakes and pâtisserie.

A colour photograph illustrates each recipe so that you can see the result you are aiming for. Important decorating and finishing touches are also highlighted in the photographs as well as in the Cook's Tips.

Here, in the Introduction, many of the basic recipes used throughout the book are grouped together for quick and easy reference.

Choose from nearly 300 appetizing recipes to find the right one for every occasion, be it a bread for breakfast, a family cake for elevenses, a biscuit for a packed lunch box, a tea-time pastry, elegant gâteaux for a special dinner party menu or a novelty cake for a celebratory party.

BASIC FRUIT CAKE

250 g/9 oz butter
275 g/10 oz soft brown sugar
1 tablespoon black treacle
6 eggs
300 g/11 oz plain flour
1 ½ teaspoons ground mixed spice
¼ teaspoon grated nutmeg
75 g/3 oz ground almonds
grated rind of 2 lemons
grated rind of 2 oranges
100 g/4 oz chopped almonds
100 g/4 oz glacé cherries
175 g/6 oz raisins
300 g/11 oz sultanas
450 g/1 lb currants
100 g/4 oz chopped mixed peel
3 tablespoons brandy
2 tablespoons orange juice

Cream the butter and sugar until light and fluffy. Beat in the treacle. Add the eggs, one at a time, adding a little of the flour with each egg after the first. Mix the flour with all the remaining ingredients except the brandy and orange juice, and gradually fold into the creamed mixture. Stir in the brandy and orange juice. Place in a 23 cm/9 inch square or 30 cm/10 inch round deep cake tin greased and lined with double greaseproof paper. Protect the outside of the tin with newspaper and bake at 140C/275G/gas 1 for 3-5 hours, checking after the first 3 hours, then at intervals after that. Allow the cake to cool in the tin for 15 minutes before turning out to cool on a wire rack.

WHISKED SPONGE

3 eggs
100 g/4 oz caster sugar
75 g/3 oz plain flour, sifted
½ teaspoon baking powder

Place the eggs and sugar in a heatproof bowl over a pan of simmering water and whisk until the mixture is thick and pale. Remove from the heat and whisk until cool. Fold in the flour then turn into a 23 cm/9 inch moule à la manque tin or cake tin. Bake at 190C/375F/gas 5 for 35-40 minutes. Turn on to a wire rack to cool. Use as required.

CHOUX PASTRY

150 g/5 oz plain flour
pinch of salt
100 g/4 oz butter
250 ml/8 fl oz water
4 eggs, beaten

Sift the flour and salt together and set aside. Melt the butter in a pan. Add the water and bring to the boil. Add the flour all at once and beat until the mixture leaves the sides of the pan. Cool slightly, then add the eggs a little at a time, beating vigorously. Use as required.

SHORTCRUST PASTRY

225 g/8 oz plain flour
pinch of salt
50 g/2 oz lard
50 g/2 oz butter or margarine
3 tablespoons cold water

Sift the flour and salt into a bowl. Rub in the lard and butter until the mixture resembles fine breadcrumbs. Add the water and bind to a firm but pliable dough. Use as required.

RICH SHORTCRUST PASTRY

250 g/10 oz plain flour
175 g/6 oz butter
2 tablespoons caster sugar
1 egg yolk, beaten with 1 tablespoon cold water

Sift the flour into a bowl and rub in the butter until the mixture resembles fine breadcrumbs. Stir in the sugar and add enough egg yolk mixture to make a firm dough. Knead lightly until smooth, wrap in clingfilm and chill for 30 minutes. Use as required.

BASIC FLAKY PASTRY

350 g/12 oz plain flour
pinch of salt
50 g/2 oz lard, chilled
175 g/6 oz butter, chilled and cut into
    5 mm/¼ inch dice
about 6 tablespoons iced water

Sift the flour and salt into a bowl and rub in the lard. Add the diced butter and rub it until the mixture resembles fine breadcrumbs. Sprinkle on the water and mix with a knife to a smooth dough. Turn onto a flat surface and shape into a flat disc. Wrap in clingfilm and chill for 1 hour. Use as required.

CREME PATISSIERE

Makes about 450 ml/¾ pint
300 ml/½ pint milk
50 g/2 oz caster sugar
20 g/¾ oz plain flour
15 g/½ oz cornflour
1 egg
1 egg yolk
few drops of vanilla essence
15-25 g/½-1 oz butter

Heat the milk gently in a saucepan but do not boil.

Put the sugar, flour, cornflour, egg and egg yolk into a bowl and whisk or heat until very smooth and creamy. Beat in a little of the hot milk.

Add the egg mixture to the rest of the milk in the pan and beat until smooth, then cook gently, stirring continuously, until the mixture thickens and comes just to the boil.

Add the vanilla essence and butter and cook gently over a low heat or a minute or so, still continuing to stir.

Remove from the heat and turn into a bowl. Cover tightly with ling film, or put a piece of wet greaseproof paper on to the surface of the custard to prevent a skin forming. The custard can be stored in the refrigerator for up to 48 hours before use, preferably in an airtight plastic container.

ALMOND PASTE

550 g/1 ¼ lb ground almonds
275 g/10 oz icing sugar
275 g/10 oz caster sugar
2 teaspoons lemon juice
few drops almond essence
few drops of orange flower water
2 eggs

Place the ground almonds, icing and caster sugar in a bowl and mix well. Add the lemon juice, almond essence, orange flower water and sufficient egg to form a stiff but manageable paste. Knead together with the fingers until smooth.

Enough to cover a 30 cm/10 inch round cake or 23 cm/9 inch square cake.

APRICOT GLAZE

25 g/8 oz apricot jam
3 tablespoons water
squeeze of lemon juice

Place the jam and water in a pan and heat until dissolved. Add the lemon juice, then sieve and return to the pan. Bring to the boil and simmer until syrupy. Use while still warm.

AMERICAN FROSTING

1 egg white
175 g/6 oz icing sugar
1 tablespoon golden syrup
3 tablespoons water
pinch of salt
1 teaspoon lemon juice

Place all the ingredients in a bowl over a pan of hot water and whisk until the icing stands in peaks. Remove from the heat and continue whisking until cool. Use at once.

BUTTER ICING

75 g/3 oz butter or margarine
225 g/8 oz icing sugar
2 tablespoons milk

Place all the ingredients in a mixing bowl and beat together with a wooden spoon until creamy.

Variations
Coffee:
Replace 1 tablespoon milk with 1 tablespoon coffee essence or 1 table spoon instant coffee dissolved in 1 tablespoon boiling water. Cool before adding to the icing.
Lemon:
Substitute lemon juice for the milk.
Orange:
Substitute orange juice for them milk.
Chocolate:
Replace 1 tablespoon milk with 1 tablespoon cocoa powder blended with 2 tablespoons hot water.

CHOCOLATE FUDGE ICING

50 g/2 oz butter or margarine
1 tablespoon milk
1 tablespoon cocoa powder
2 tablespoons hot water
225 g/8 oz icing sugar, sifted

Place the butter, milk, cocoa powder dissolved in the hot water and icing sugar in a bowl over a pan of hot water. Stir until smooth and glossy. Remove from the heat and allow to cool. Beat well with a wooden spoon until thick enough to spread.

SATIN ICING

50 g/2 oz butter or margarine
4 tablespoons lemon juice
about 675 g/1½ lb icing sugar, sifted
few drops of food colouring (optional)

Warm the butter and lemon juice in a pan until melted. Add 225 g/8 oz of the icing sugar and heat gently, stirring, until dissolved. Increase the heat slightly and simmer gently for 2 minutes; do not overboil at this stage or the icing will be too hard. Remove from the heat and add a further 225 g/8 oz of the icing sugar. Beat thoroughly with a wooden spoon, then turn into a mixing bowl. Gradually mix in enough of the remaining icing sugar to give a soft dough. Turn on to a surface dusted with icing sugar and knead until smooth, adding colouring if used. Use to mould decorations or to cover the top and sides of a cake. If wrapped in clingfilm, this icing will keep in the refrigerator for up to 6 weeks.

GLACE ICING

approx 1 tablespoon water
100 g/4 oz icing sugar, sifted

Stir the water into the icing sugar very gradually, and mix to a spreading consistency, adding a little more water if necessary. Beat until smooth.

For a thinner icing, mix to a pouring consistence, adding ½ teaspoon water at a time. For a very thin, transparent icing continue adding the water very carefully. Flavour and colour to taste.

Chocolate:
Sift 1 tablespoon cocoa with the icing sugar and mix with black coffee or water.
Coffee:
Sift 2 teaspoons instant coffee powder with the icing sugar and mix with black coffee instead of water.
Lemon:
Mix with strained lemon juice instead of water. Tint yellow with a few drops of yellow colouring, if liked.
Lemon curd:
Beat 3-4 teaspoon lemon curd with the basic mixture.
Orange:
Use orange juice instead of water to mix and tint with a few drops of orange colouring, if liked.

Peppermint:
Add a few drops of peppermint oil the basic mixture and tint a delicate green.
Vanilla;
Add a few drops of vanilla essence to the basic mixture and tint pink with a few drops of cochineal, if liked.

ROYAL ICING

4 egg whites
1 kg/2 lb icing sugar, sifted
2 teaspoons glycerine
few drops of rose water

Place the egg whites in a bowl and whisk until frothy. Gradually add the icing sugar, beating well between additions, until the icing is shiny and very white. Finally beat in the glycerine and rose water. Enough to cover the top and sides of a 30 cm/10 inch round cake or 23 cm/9 inch square cake.

NOTES FOR AMERICAN AND AUSTRALIAN USERS

In America the 8 fl oz measuring cup is used. In Australia metric measures are now used in conjunction with the standard 250 ml measuring cup. The Imperial pint, used in Britain and Australia, is 20 fl oz, while the American pint is 16 fl oz. It is important to remember that the Australian tablespoon differs from both the British and American tablespoons; the table below gives a comparison. The British standard tablespoon, which has been used throughout this book, holds 17.7 ml, the American 14.2 ml, and the Australian 20 ml. A teaspoon holds approximately 5 ml in all three countries.

British	American	Australian
1 teaspoon	1 teaspoon	1 teaspoon
1 tablespoon	1 tablespoon	1 tablespoon
2 tablespoons	3 tablespoons	2 tablespoons
3½ tablespoons	4 tablespoons	3 tablespoons
4 tablespoons	5 tablespoons	3½ tablespoons

An Imperial/American guide to solid and liquid measures

Imperial	American
Solid measures	
1lb butter or margarine	2 cups
1lb flour	4 cups
1lb granulated or caster sugar	2 cups
1lb icing sugar	3 cups
8 oz rice	1 cup
Liquid measures	
¼ pint liquid	⅔ cup liquid
½ pint	1¼ cups
¾ pint	2 cups
1 pint	2½ cups
1½ pints	3¾ cups
2 pints	5 cups (2½ pints)

Note: When making any of the recipes in this book, only follow one set of measurements as they are not interchangeable.

BREADS

There is more here than the traditional baker's dozen of breads, for a selection of rolls, muffins and small, shaped loaves has been included as well. It is a good idea to plan for a day's baking, since breads can be baked in bulk and then frozen. They may be quickly thawed, then refreshed in a hot oven for same-day baked freshness.

1 GRANARY BREAD

Preparation time:
20 minutes, plus proving

Cooking time:
35-40 minutes

Oven temperature:
220C/425F/gas 7
190C/375F/gas 5

Makes 2 round loaves

Calories:
1429 per loaf

YOU WILL NEED:
1 tablespoon dried yeast
1 teaspoon caster sugar
450 ml/¾ pint warm water and
milk mixed
275 g/10 oz plain wholemeal flour
275 g/10 oz strong plain white flour
1 tablespoon salt
15 g/½ oz butter or margarine
150 g/5 oz cracked wheat
50 g/2 oz wheatgerm
2 tablespoons malt extract

Mix the yeast, sugar, water and milk mixture and leave for 10 minutes. Sift the flours and salt into a bowl. Rub in the butter or margarine. Mix in 100 g/4 oz of the cracked wheat and the wheatgerm. Add the yeast liquid and malt extract and mix to a smooth dough. Turn on to a floured surface and knead for 5 minutes until smooth and elastic. Place in a clean, oiled bowl, cover and leave to rise in a warm place for 1 hour.

Knead for a few minutes, divide in half and shape into rounds. Place on greased baking trays. Cover and leave in a warm place for 30 minutes until doubled in size, then sprinkle with the remaining cracked wheat.

Bake at the higher temperature for 15 minutes then the lower for 20-25 minutes. Cool on a wire rack.

◼ COOK'S TIP

Granary bread freezes successfully for up to 3 months. Open freeze until firm, then wrap in foil or freezer film. Remove, unwrap and thaw slowly at cool room temperature, then refresh the loaf or loaves in a hot oven for same-day baked freshness.

2 CRUSTY FRENCH LOAVES

Preparation time:
20 minutes, plus proving

Cooking time:
22-25 minutes

Oven temperature:
220C/425F/gas 7

Makes 2 loaves

Calories:
823 per loaf

YOU WILL NEED:
2 teaspoons dried yeast
300 ml/½ pint warm water
1 teaspoon caster sugar
400 g/14 oz plain flour
50 g/2 oz cornflour
1 teaspoon salt
beaten egg to glaze
poppy seeds (optional)

Mix the yeast, water and sugar and leave for 10 minutes. Sift the flours and salt into a bowl. Gradually add the yeast liquid and mix to a dough. Turn on to a floured surface and knead for 5-10 minutes until smooth and elastic. Place in a clean, oiled bowl, cover and leave to rise in a warm place for 1 hour.

Knead for a few minutes, divide in half and roll each piece to a 35 x 15 cm/14 x 6 in oblong with rounded ends. Roll up from the long side like a Swiss roll and place, seam-side down, on a floured baking tray. Slash with a sharp knife at regular intervals. Mix a pinch of salt with the egg and glaze the loaves. Leave in a warm place for 30 minutes until doubled in size.

Sprinkle with poppy seeds if liked and bake for 22-25 minutes until crisp and brown. Cool on a wire rack.

◼ COOK'S TIP

If a softer French loaf is liked, place a roasting tin of hot water in the bottom of the oven during baking. The steam produced will help to keep the crust a little softer.

3   POPPYSEED LOAVES

Preparation time:
20 minutes

Cooking time:
1¼ hours

Oven temperature:
160C/325F/gas 3

Makes 2 x 1 kg/2 lb loaves

Calories:
4172 per loaf

YOU WILL NEED:
4 eggs, beaten
450 g/1 lb sugar
300 ml/½ pint corn oil
675 g/1½ lb plain flour
1 x 397 g/14 oz can condensed milk
1 teaspoon vanilla essence
1½ teaspoons bicarbonate of soda
1 teaspoon salt
5 tablespoons poppyseeds

Mix the eggs with the sugar, corn oil, flour, condensed milk, vanilla essence, bicarbonate of soda, salt and half of the poppyseeds. Divide the mixture evenly between two greased and floured 1 kg/2 lb loaf tins. Sprinkle with the remaining poppyseeds.

Bake for 1¼ hours until well risen and golden. Remove from the tins and cool on a wire rack.

This is a rich and sweet bread that is ideal to serve lightly buttered or toasted at teatime.

4   BASIC WHITE BREAD

Preparation time:
20 minutes, plus proving

Cooking time:
35-40 minutes

Oven temperature:
220C/425F/gas 7

Makes 2 x 1 kg/2 lb loaves

Calories:
2450 per loaf

YOU WILL NEED:
25 g/1 oz fresh yeast
1 teaspoon caster sugar
900 ml/1½ pints warm water
1.5 kg/3 lb strong white plain flour
1 tablespoon salt
1 tablespoon oil
flour to sprinkle

Cream the yeast with the sugar and a little of the water and leave for 10 minutes. Sift the flour and salt into a bowl. Pour in the yeast, remaining water and oil. Mix to a smooth dough.

Turn on to a floured surface and knead for 8-10 minutes until smooth and elastic. Place in a clean, warmed bowl, cover with a damp cloth and leave to rise in a warm place for 2 hours until doubled in size.

Knead on a floured surface for a few minutes, divide in half and place in two greased 1 kg/2 lb loaf tins. Cover and leave in a warm place for 30 minutes until risen to the tops of the tins.

Sprinkle with flour and bake for 35-40 minutes. Cool on a wire rack.

▨ COOK'S TIP

If a loaf such as this one begins to brown too much before it is fully cooked, cover it loosely with a piece of foil for the remainder of the cooking time.

▨ COOK'S TIP

Glazing with beaten egg gives a golden look and brushing with milk or dusting with flour gives a soft bap-like appearance to the top of the bread.

5 WHOLEMEAL BREAD

Preparation time:
20 minutes, plus
proving

Cooking time:
30-40 minutes

Oven temperature:
220C/425F/gas 7

**Makes 4 x 450 g/1
lb loaves**

Calories:
316 per loaf

YOU WILL NEED:
1.5 kg/3 lb wholemeal flour
1 tablespoon salt
25 g/1 oz butter
25 g/1 oz fresh yeast
900 ml-1.5 litres/1½-2 pints
    warm water
2 tablespoons malt extract
cracked wheat, to sprinkle

Mix the flour and salt and rub in the butter. Mix the yeast with a little of the water and leave for 10 minutes. Mix the malt extract with the remaining water, add to the flour with the yeast and mix to a dough.

Knead for 8-10 minutes until smooth and elastic. Place in a clean, warmed bowl, cover with a damp cloth and leave to rise in a warm place for 2 hours until doubled in size.

Knead for a few minutes, divide into 4 pieces and place in greased 450 g/1 lb loaf tins or clay flowerpots. Brush with water and sprinkle with cracked wheat. Cover and leave in a warm place for 30 minutes until risen to the top of the tins or flowerpots.

Bake for 30-40 minutes. Cool on a wire rack.

6 WHOLEMEAL SODA BREAD

Preparation time:
20 minutes

Cooking time:
25-30 minutes

Oven temperature:
220C/425F/gas 7

**Makes 1 675 g/1½ lb
loaf**

Total calories:
2046

YOU WILL NEED:
225 g/8 oz plain flour
1 teaspoon bicarbonate of soda
2 teaspoons cream of tartar
2 teaspoons salt
350 g/12 oz wholemeal flour
300 ml/½ pint milk
4 tablespoons water
flour, to sprinkle

Sift the plain flour, bicarbonate of soda, cream of tartar and salt into a mixing bowl. Stir in the wholemeal flour, then add the milk and water and mix to a soft dough.

Turn on to a floured surface, knead lightly, then shape into a large round about 5 cm/2 in thick.

Place on a floured baking tray, cut a deep cross in the top of the loaf and sprinkle with flour. Bake for 25-30 minutes. Cool on a wire rack.

▨ COOK'S TIP

Season a new clay flowerpot by brushing the inside thoroughly with oil. Put the pot in a moderately hot oven for 15 minutes. Allow to cool completely.

▨ COOK'S TIP

To cook in a microwave, place on a large greased plate. Microwave on Medium (50%) power for 5 minutes, giving the plate a half turn twice. Increase the *power setting to Full (100%) and microwave for a further 3 minutes, giving the plate a half-turn twice. Allow to stand for 10 minutes before cooling.*

7 HERB SODA BREAD ROLLS

Preparation time:	YOU WILL NEED:
15 minutes	225 g/8 oz wholemeal flour
	225 g/8 oz plain flour
Cooking time:	2 teaspoons salt
20 minutes	1 teaspoon bicarbonate of soda
	50 g/2 oz butter or margarine
Oven temperature:	100 g/4 oz grated onion
200C/400F/gas 6	100 g/4 oz grated celery
	2 tablespoons chopped parsley
Makes 8 rolls	1 tablespoon chopped fresh mint
	or chervil
Calories:	3 teaspoons lemon juice
299 per roll	275 ml/9 fl oz milk
	milk and sesame or poppy seeds,
	to top

Sift the flours, salt and bicarbonate of soda into a mixing bowl. Cut the fat into the flour and rub in to a breadcrumb consistency. Add the onion, celery and herbs, rubbing in with the fingertips until thoroughly mixed. Stir the lemon juice into the milk and mix to a soft dough with the dry ingredients.

Turn on to a well floured board and knead lightly into a smooth round ball. Pinch off pieces weighing about 75 g/3 oz each and roll into balls. Place on a warmed, floured baking tray leaving room between for expansion. Flatten the tops, brush with milk and sprinkle thickly with poppy or sesame seeds. Bake near the top of the oven for 20 minutes, or until well risen and golden brown. Cook on a wire rack.

◼ COOK'S TIP

*Butter the freshly baked rolls
and fill with watercress,
lettuce and tomato, ham
or cheeses. Any stale rolls
can be served toasted with
a cheese topping.*

8 LIGHT RYE BREAD

Preparation time:	YOU WILL NEED:
20 minutes, plus	675 g/1½ lb white rye flour
proving	2 teaspoons caster sugar
	2 x 25 mg ascorbic acid tablets
Cooking time:	450 ml/¾ pint warm water
50 minutes	1 tablespoon dried yeast
	2 teaspoons salt
Oven temperature:	2 tablespoons caraway seeds
180C/350F/gas 4	knob of butter
	1 teaspoon cornflour mixed with a
Makes 2 x 450 g/1	little water to glaze
lb loaves	
Calories:	
1204 per loaf	

Sift 225 g/8 oz of the flour and the sugar into a bowl. Add the ascorbic acid tablets, water and yeast and mix until smooth. Leave in a warm place for 1 hour.

Sift the remaining flour and the salt into another bowl. Add the caraway seeds and rub in the butter. Add the risen yeast batter and mix to a soft dough. Knead on a floured surface for 5 minutes until smooth and elastic. Place in a clean, warmed bowl, cover and leave to rise in a warm place for 1 -1½ hours until doubled in size.

Knead for a few minutes, divide in half and shape into smooth balls. Place on greased baking trays, cover and leave in a warm place until doubled in size.

Bake for 30 minutes, brush with the cornflour glaze and bake for a further 20 minutes. Cool on a wire rack.

◼ COOK'S TIP

*Ascorbic acid tablets can be
bought from chemists or
can occasionally be
purchased from
supermarkets.*

9   COTTAGE MILK LOAF

Preparation time:
25 minutes, plus rising

Cooking time:
35-40 minutes

Oven temperature:
230C/450F/gas 8

Makes 1 large loaf

Total calories:
3122

YOU WILL NEED:
450 ml/¾ pint warm milk
1 teaspoon sugar
2 teaspoons dried yeast
675 g/1½ lb white bread flour
2 teaspoons salt
25 g/1 oz caster sugar
75 g/3 oz butter or margarine
beaten egg or milk, to glaze

Pour the milk into a bowl. Sprinkle over the sugar and yeast. Leave until frothy, about 10 minutes. Put the flour, salt and sugar in a bowl and rub in the fat. Add the yeast liquid and mix to a soft dough. Turn on to a floured surface and knead until silky and no longer sticky. Place in an oiled polythene bag and leave until doubled in size, about 1 hour. Turn out on to a floured surface and knead for 2 minutes.

Remove one-third of the dough. Shape the larger piece into a round and place on a greased baking tray. Then shape the small piece into a round and place on top. Press a floured wooden spoon handle through the centre of the dough, to the bottom. Cover with oiled polythene and leave to rise until doubled in size, about 45 minutes.

Brush with the beaten egg or milk and bake for 35-40 minutes until deep golden brown and the bread sounds hollow when tapped on the base. Cool on a wire rack.

▮ COOK'S TIP

Kneading dough strengthens the gluten element in the flour, which forms tiny bubbles filled with carbon dioxide released by the yeast.

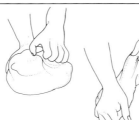

10   CHEESE AND HERB BREAD

Preparation time:
20 minutes, plus rising

Cooking time:
35-40 minutes

Oven temperature:
230C/450F/gas 8

Makes 1 large loaf

Total calories:
2213

YOU WILL NEED:
25 g/1 oz butter
1 small onion, chopped
300 ml/½ pint warm water
1 teaspoon sugar
2 teaspoons dried yeast
450 g/1 lb wheatmeal flour
1½ teaspoons salt
1 teaspoon dry mustard
2 teaspoons mixed dried herbs or
    1 tablespoon freshly chopped herbs
125 g/4½ oz Cheddar cheese,
    finely grated

Melt the butter in a small pan, add the onion and fry until softened, about 5 minutes. Measure the water into a jug. Sprinkle over the sugar and yeast. Leave until frothy, about 10 minutes.

Put the flour, salt, mustard, herbs and 100 g/4 oz of the cheese in a mixing bowl. Add the onions and mix well. Add the yeast liquid and mix to a soft dough.

Turn on to a floured surface and knead for about 5 minutes. Shape into an oblong and place in a greased 1 kg/2 lb loaf tin. Cover with oiled polythene and leave to rise until doubled in size, about 35 minutes.

Sprinkle the remaining cheese over the top. Bake for 35-40 minutes, until golden brown and the bread sounds hollow when tapped on the base. Serve warm with butter.

▮ COOK'S TIP

Try different combinations of strongly flavoured fresh herbs. Snipped chives go well with cheese, so does oregano or marjoram.

11　QUICK WHEATMEAL BREAD

Preparation time:
10 minutes, plus rising

Cooking time:
30 minutes

Oven temperature:
230C/450F/gas 8

Makes 1 round loaf

Total calories:
1665

YOU WILL NEED:
300 ml/½ pint warm water
2 teaspoons dried yeast
2 teaspoons sugar
450 g/1 lb wheatmeal flour
1½ teaspoons salt
15 g/½ oz butter, margarine or lard
cracked wheat or oats, to sprinkle

Measure the warm water into a jug. Sprinkle over the yeast and 1 teaspoon of the sugar and leave for about 10 minutes, until frothy. Place the flour, salt and remaining sugar in a mixing bowl and rub in the fat. Pour the yeast liquid, all at once, into the flour and mix to a soft dough.

Turn the dough on to a floured surface and knead for 5 minutes, until smooth and no longer sticky. Shape the dough into a round and place on a greased baking sheet. Cut a deep cross in the top with a sharp knife. Cover with oiled polythene and leave until doubled in size, about 30 minutes.

Remove the polythene and brush with water. Sprinkle with the cracked wheat or oats. Bake for 30 minutes until brown and crisp and the bread sounds hollow when tapped on the base. Cool on a wire rack.

▨ COOK'S TIP

To make rolls, divide the dough into 12 equal pieces. Shape into balls and place apart on a greased baking sheet. Leave to rise as above and bake for 12-15 minutes *at the same temperature as above.*

12　CURRANT BREAD

Preparation time:
25 minutes, plus rising

Cooking time:
35-40 minutes

Oven temperature:
200C/400F/gas 6

Makes 1 large loaf

Total calories:
2437

YOU WILL NEED:
300 ml/½ pint warm milk
1 teaspoon sugar
2 teaspoons dried yeast
450 g/1 lb white bread flour
1 teaspoon salt
25 g/1 oz caster sugar
25 g/1 oz butter
100 g/4 oz currants
clear honey, to glaze

Measure the milk into a jug. Sprinkle over the sugar and yeast and leave until frothy, about 10 minutes. Mix the flour, salt and sugar in a bowl and rub in the butter. Add the yeast liquid and mix to a soft dough.

Turn on to a floured surface. Knead until smooth, silky and no longer sticky, about 10 minutes. Place in an oiled polythene bag and leave until doubled in size, about 1 hour.

Turn on to a floured surface and beat the dough with the fists to remove the air bubbles. Knead the currants into the dough. Shape into an oblong and place in a greased 1 kg/2 lb loaf tin. Cover with oiled polythene and leave until doubled in size, about 40 minutes.

Bake for 35-40 minutes, until deep golden brown and the bread sounds hollow when tapped on the base. Cool on a wire rack. Brush with honey while still warm. Serve sliced and buttered.

▨ COOK'S TIP

If the currants look very dry and shrivelled, try plumping them up in a microwave. Place in a dish, cover with water and cook on full power for 5 minutes. Then *stir, leave to stand for 5 minutes and drain well.*

13 GRANARY TWISTS

Preparation time:
25 minutes, plus rising

Cooking time:
30-35 minutes

Oven temperature:
230C/459F/gas 8

Makes 2 loaves

Calories:
1271 per loaf

YOU WILL NEED:
450 ml/¾ pint warm water
1 teaspoon sugar
2 teaspoons dried yeast
675 g/1½ lb granary flour
2 teaspoons salt
25 g/1 oz butter, margarine or lard
granary flour, for sprinkling

Measure the water into a jug. Sprinkle over the sugar and yeast and leave until frothy, about 10 minutes.

Put the flour and salt in a bowl and rub in the fat. Add the yeast liquid and mix to a soft dough. Turn on to a floured surface and knead until no longer sticky. Place in a large oiled polythene bag and leave until doubled in size, about 1 hour.

Turn out on to a floured surface, punch the dough, then knead again for 2 minutes. Divide the dough in half. Divide each piece in half again and shape into four sausages about 30 cm/12 inches long. Twist two of the sausages together and place on a greased baking sheet. Repeat with the other two. Sprinkle with granary flour and cover with oiled polythene. Leave to rise for 30-40 minutes, until doubled in size.

Bake for 30-35 minutes until the bread sounds hollow when tapped on the base. Cool on a wire rack.

■ COOK'S TIP

Wholemeal and brown flours have a higher fat content than white flour so they may become rancid if kept for too long. Always store flour in a cool, well-ventilated place.

14 SCOTS BAPS

Preparation time:
20 minutes, plus rising

Cooking time:
15-20 minutes

Oven temperature:
220C/425F/gas 7

Makes 10

Calories:
166 per portion

YOU WILL NEED:
450 g/1 lb strong white flour
2 teaspoons salt
150 ml/¼ pint warm milk
150 ml/¼ pint warm water
15 g/½ oz fresh yeast
milk and flour, to glaze

Sift the flour and salt into a mixing bowl and leave in a warm place. Mix the milk and water together and blend in the yeast. Leave for 10 minutes to froth, then stir into the flour. Mix well to a soft slack dough, adding a little warm water if necessary.

Turn on to a floured board and knead for 4-5 minutes until the dough no longer sticks. Cover the bowl with oiled polythene and leave to rise for 1½ hours or until the dough springs back when pressed.

Knead the dough lightly and press it out by hand until 1.5 cm/½ inch thick. Divide into 10 equal-sized pieces and shape into ovals. Place on a floured baking sheet, leaving room for expansion. Cover and prove for 15 minutes.

Brush tops and sides with milk and sprinkle with flour. Press 3 floured fingers into the centre of each bap to prevent blistering. Bake in the centre of the oven for 15-20 minutes, until well risen and golden brown. Dust with flour.

■ COOK'S TIP

Traditionally served for breakfast in Scotland, these are best served hot from the oven and spread with butter and honey or marmalade.

15   KENTISH HUFFKINS

Preparation time:
20 minutes, plus rising

Cooking time:
20 minutes

Oven temperature:
230C/450F/gas 8

Makes 8

Calories:
357 per portion

YOU WILL NEED:
1 tablespoon dried yeast
1 teaspoon caster sugar
450 ml/¾ pint warm water and
  milk mixed
675 g/1½lb strong plain white flour
1½ teaspoons salt
50 g/2 oz lard

Mix the yeast with the sugar and half the water and milk mixture and leave for 10 minutes. Sift the flour and salt into a bowl, then rub in the lard. Add the yeast and remaining milk mixture and mix to a soft dough. Knead on a lightly floured surface for 5-10 minutes until smooth and elastic. Place in a bowl, cover and leave to rise in a warm place for 1 hour until doubled in size.

Knead on a floured surface for a few minutes, divide into 8 pieces and shape each into a smooth ball. Flatten to 2.5 cm/1 in thick with a rolling pin and place on greased baking trays. Cover and leave in a warm place for 45-50 minutes until doubled in size.

Bake for 10 minutes, then turn over with a spatula and bake for a further 10 minutes. Remove and leave to cool on a wire rack, covered with a clean teatowel.

▨ COOK'S TIP

Covering the huffkins with a teatowel after cooking helps achieve the soft outer crust typical of these bread rolls. Split them and and fill with savoury fillings.

16   LIGHT BROWN BAPS

Preparation time:
20 minutes, plus rising

Cooking time:
15-20 minutes

Oven temperature:
200C/400F/gas 6

Makes 12

Calories:
187 per portion

YOU WILL NEED:
350 ml/12 fl oz milk
1 teaspoon caster sugar
2 teaspoons dried yeast
225 g/8 oz strong plain white flour
225 g/8 oz plain wholemeal flour
1 teaspoon salt
50 g/2 oz lard
flour, to dust

Mix the milk with the sugar and yeast and leave for 10 minutes. Sift the flours and salt into a bowl, then rub in the lard. Add the yeast and mix to a soft dough.

Turn on to a floured surface and knead for 5-10 minutes until smooth and elastic. Place in an oiled bowl, cover and leave to rise in a warm place for 1 hour until doubled in size.

Knead for a few minutes, then divide and shape into 12 baps, floured on all sides. Place, well apart, on greased baking trays, cover and leave in a warm place to rise until doubled in size.

Dust with extra flour and slash the top of each bap. Bake for 15-20 minutes. Cool on a wire rack.

▨ COOK'S TIP

These baps can be frozen before proving and baking for convenience if liked. Thaw completely, about 1-2 hours, then prove as above before baking.

17 QUICK AND EASY CELERY LUNCH LOAF

Preparation time:
20 minutes

Cooking time:
45-50 minutes

Oven temperature:
190C/375F/gas 5

Makes 1 cob loaf

Total calories:
1451

YOU WILL NEED:
225 g/8 oz self-raising flour
½ teaspoon salt
¼ teaspoon cayenne pepper
25 g/1 oz butter or margarine
100 g/4 oz celery heart, finely chopped
100 g/4 oz Edam cheese, grated
1 tablespoon snipped chives
150 ml/¼ pint milk

Sift the flour, salt and cayenne pepper into a bowl. Rub in the butter, then stir in the celery, Edam and chives. Add the milk and mix to a soft dough. Turn on to a lightly floured surface and knead until smooth.

Shape into a cob by drawing the dough upwards and into the centre. Place tucks-side down on a greased baking tray and slash the top with a sharp knife.

Bake for 45-50 minutes. Cover the loaf with a little foil towards the end of the cooking time if the crust is browning too much. Cool on a wire rack. Serve sliced while still warm.

18 FRENCH BRIOCHES

Preparation time:
20 minutes, plus rising

Cooking time:
10 minutes

Oven temperature:
230C/450F/gas 8

Makes 12

Calories:
122 per portion

YOU WILL NEED:
1 tablespoon dried yeast
1½ tablespoons warm water
1 tablespoon caster sugar
225 g/8 oz strong plain white flour
½ teaspoon salt
2 eggs, beaten
50 g/2 oz butter, melted
beaten egg, to glaze

Mix the yeast with the water and 1 teaspoon of the sugar and leave for 10 minutes. Sift the flour, salt and remaining sugar into a bowl. Add the yeast mixture, eggs and butter and mix to a smooth dough. Knead on a floured surface for 5 minutes until smooth and elastic. Place in an oiled bowl, cover and leave to rise in a warm place for 1 hour until doubled in size.

Knead for a few minutes, then divide into 12 pieces. Shape three-quarters of each into a round and place in an oiled 7.5 cm/3 in fluted patty tin. Press a hole in the centre. Shape the remaining one-quarter into a ball and place on top. Cover and leave in a warm place to rise until the dough reaches the top of the tins.

Brush with beaten egg and bake for 10 minutes. Cool on a wire rack. The brioches are best eaten on the day of making.

■ COOK'S TIP

If liked, add 25 g/1 oz cooked chopped bacon with the celery. This versatile lunch loaf can also be made with a finely chopped green pepper instead of the celery.

■ COOK'S TIP

Brioches freeze beautifully for up to 3 months and so are worth making in bulk. Open freeze until firm, then wrap in foil or freezer film or place in a freezer box.

Thaw at room temperature, then reheat in a moderate oven (180C/350F/gas 4) for a few minutes to refresh.

19   ENGLISH MUFFINS

Preparation time:
20 minutes, plus rising

Cooking time:
15-16 minutes

Oven temperature:
230C/450F/gas 8

Makes 8-10

Calories:
266 - 205 per
portion

YOU WILL NEED:
1 tablespoon dried yeast
½ teaspoon caster sugar
300 ml/½ pint warm milk
1 egg, beaten
25 g/1 oz butter, melted
450 g/1 lb plain flour
1 teaspoon salt

Mix the yeast with the sugar and half of the milk and leave for 10 minutes. Mix the egg with the remaining milk and butter. Sift the flour and salt into a bowl. Add the yeast and egg mixtures and mix to a soft dough.

Turn on to a lightly floured surface and knead for about 5 minutes until smooth and elastic. Place in an oiled bowl, cover and leave to rise for about 1½ hours in a warm place until doubled in size.

Roll out the dough on a floured surface and stamp out 8-10 rounds with a 7.5 cm/3 in scone or biscuit cutter. Place on greased baking trays and bake for 8 minutes. Turn over with a spatula and bake for a further 7-8 minutes. Cool on a wire rack. Serve split and toasted, with butter.

■ COOK'S TIP

Dried yeast, unlike fresh yeast, will keep for many months but it needs to be activated with sugar and water before use. Both types can be used in all *bread recipes but remember when using dried yeast to use only half the quantity specified for fresh.*

20   MUSTARD, WALNUT AND BACON FLOWERPOTS

Preparation time:
20 minutes, plus
rising

Cooking time:
35 minutes

Oven temperature:
220C/425F/gas 7

Makes 4

Calories:
941 per flowerpot

YOU WILL NEED:
550 ml/18 fl oz warm water
4 tablespoons Dijon mustard
1 tablespoon plus pinch of caster
  sugar
1 tablespoon dried yeast
750 g/1 lb 10 oz wheatmeal flour
2 teaspoons salt
25 g/1 oz lard
100 g/4 oz walnuts, chopped
100 g/4 oz bacon, cooked and
  chopped
beaten egg ,to glaze
toasted barley flakes, to sprinkle

Mix the water with the mustard. Mix half the mustard water with the pinch of sugar and yeast and leave for 10 minutes. Sift the flour, remaining sugar and salt into a bowl. Rub in the lard, then stir in the walnuts and bacon. Add the yeast and remaining mustard water and mix to a smooth dough. Knead on a floured surface for 10 minutes until smooth. Place in a bowl, cover and leave in a warm place until doubled in size.

Knead on a floured surface for a few minutes, divide into 4 pieces and shape to fit 4 750 ml/1¼ pint tall well-greased clay flowerpots. Cover and leave in a warm place until the dough almost fills the pots.

Slash the tops with a sharp knife, glaze with egg and sprinkle with barley flakes. Bake for 35 minutes.

■ COOK'S TIP

You may substitute pecans for the walnuts in this recipe. They have a milder yet equally nutty flavour.

SCONES, BUNS & TEABREADS

Traditional scones and buns from all over Britain join with teabreads from Britain and abroad to make a splendidly varied chapter of small 'plain baking'. Some of the buns here need as long proving as bread, while others can be mixed and put into the oven in just 10 minutes, making them ideal for quickly-made teatime treats.

21 BATH BUNS

Preparation time:
25 minutes, plus rising

Cooking time:
10-15 minutes

Oven temperature:
220C/425F/gas 7

Makes 12

Calories:
140 per portion

YOU WILL NEED:
125 ml/4 fl oz warm milk
1 teaspoon granulated sugar
2 teaspoons dried yeast
225 g/8 oz white bread flour
½ teaspoon salt
25 g/1 oz butter or margarine
25 g/1 oz caster sugar
75 g/3 oz sultanas
25 g/1 oz cut mixed peel
1 egg, beaten
beaten egg, to glaze
25 g/1 oz sugar cubes, crushed

Pour the milk into a bowl and sprinkle over the granulated sugar and yeast. Leave for 5 minutes, until starting to froth, then beat in 50 g/2 oz of the flour. Leave in a warm place until frothy, about 20 minutes. Mix the remaining flour and salt in a bowl and rub in the butter or margarine. Stir in the sugar, sultanas and peel. Add the flour mixture and the beaten egg to the yeast batter. Mix to a soft dough. Beat with a wooden spoon for 3 minutes. Cover the bowl and leave to rise for about 1 hour, until doubled in size. Beat again for 1 minute, then place tablespoonfuls, well apart, on greased baking trays. Brush the buns with beaten egg and sprinkle with crushed sugar cubes. Cover loosely with oiled polythene and leave to prove for about 30 minutes, until doubled in size.

Bake in the oven for 10-15 minutes, until golden brown and firm. Serve warm with butter.

22 FRUIT SCONES

Preparation time:
10-15 minutes

Cooking time:
10 minutes

Oven temperature:
220C/425F/gas 7

Makes about 12

Calories:
131 per portion

YOU WILL NEED:
225 g/8 oz self-raising flour
½ teaspoon baking powder
50 g/2 oz butter or margarine
2 tablespoons caster sugar
75 g/3 oz mixed dried fruit
about 150 ml/¼ pint milk
milk, to glaze

Sift the flour and baking powder into a bowl. Rub in the butter until the mixture resembles fine breadcrumbs. Stir in the sugar and fruit and add enough milk to mix to a soft dough.

Turn on to a floured surface, knead lightly and roll out to a 2 cm/¾ inch thickness. Cut into 5 cm/2 inch rounds and place on a lightly floured baking tray. Brush with milk to glaze.

Bake for 10 minutes, then cool on a wire rack. Serve with butter and jam.

■ COOK'S TIP

Cover yeasted buns and breads with clingfilm during proving. This prevents the dough drying out or developing a crust before further kneading.

■ COOK'S TIP

Most scones will keep for a day or two if stored in an airtight tin but are always best refreshed in the oven for a few minutes before serving.

23 CHEESE SCONES

Preparation time:	YOU WILL NEED:
15-20 minutes	225 g/8 oz plain flour
	½ teaspoon salt
Cooking time:	1 teaspoon dry mustard
10-15 minutes	4 teaspoons baking powder
	50 g/2 oz butter or margarine
Oven temperature:	75-100 g/3-4 oz mature Cheddar
220C/425F/gas 7	cheese, grated
	1 egg, beaten
Makes about 12	150 ml/¼ pint milk or water
	milk, to brush
Calories:	grated cheese, to sprinkle
160 per scone	

Sift the flour, salt, mustard and baking powder into a mixing bowl. Rub in the fat until the mixture resembles fine breadcrumbs. Mix in the grated cheese. Beat the egg with half the liquid and stir into the dry ingredients. Work into a soft dough adding more liquid as necessary.

Turn on to a well-floured board and roll out lightly to 2 cm/¾ inch thickness. Cut out rounds with a 6.5 cm/2½ inch cutter. Work the remaining dough into a round and cut into triangles. Place on a warmed baking tray. Brush with milk and sprinkle with grated cheese.

Bake for 10-15 minutes until well-risen and golden. Cool on a wire rack. Serve with butter, cream cheese, or salad filling.

24 SPICED TREACLE SCONES

Preparation time:	YOU WILL NEED:
20 minutes	225 g/8 oz plain flour
	½ teaspoon salt
Cooking time:	½ teaspoon bicarbonate of soda
12-15 minutes	1 teaspoon cream of tartar
	½ teaspoon ground cinnamon
Oven temperature:	½ teaspoon ground ginger or
230C/450F/gas 8	mixed spice
	25 g/1 oz butter or margarine
Makes about 14	25 g/1 oz caster sugar
	1 tablespoon black treacle
Calories:	125 ml/4 fl oz milk
87 per portion	milk, to glaze

Sift the flour, salt, bicarbonate of soda, cream of tartar and spices into a mixing bowl. Rub the fat in until the mixture resembles fine breadcrumbs. Mix in the sugar. Dissolve the treacle in the milk over very gentle heat, cool slightly and stir into the flour to make a soft dough. Turn on to a floured board, knead lightly until smooth. Roll out to a good 1 cm/½ inch thick piece and cut into rounds with a 5 cm/2 inch cutter. Roll the trimmings out into a round and cut across into four triangles. Place the scones on a warmed and greased baking tray and brush with milk.

Bake near the top of the oven for 12-15 minutes. Cool on a wire rack. Serve split and spread with butter.

▪ COOK'S TIP

Judge carefully the amount of milk to add to a scone mixture to achieve a soft but not sticky dough. Too much liquid will result in a sticky dough and hard, *brittle scones; too little and the scones will be dry and crumbly.*

▪ COOK'S TIP

For an unusual tea-time treat, serve these scones with ginger marmalade or finely chopped crystallized ginger mixed with cream cheese.

25   HONEY AND CREAM SCONES

Preparation time:	YOU WILL NEED:
20 minutes	*175 g/6 oz wholemeal flour*
	175 g/6 oz plain flour
Cooking time:	*2 teaspoons bicarbonate of soda*
about 10 minutes	*1 teaspoon cream of tartar*
	25 g/1 oz butter or margarine
Oven temperature:	*150 ml/¼ pint soured cream*
230C/450F/gas 8	*100 g/4 oz clear honey*
	1 egg
Makes about 12	*milk, to glaze*

Calories:
174 per portion

Sift the flour, bicarbonate of soda and cream of tartar into a mixing bowl. Rub the fat in until the mixture resembles fine breadcrumbs. Mix the soured cream and honey together until the honey is dissolved. Beat in the egg. Make a well in the flour, pour in the liquid and mix to a soft dough.

Turn on to a floured board and knead in a little extra flour if necessary. Roll out to 1 cm/½ inch thickness and cut into rounds with a 5 cm/2 inch cutter. Roll the trimmings into a round and cut into four triangles. Place on a warmed floured baking tray and brush the scones with milk.

Bake near the top of the oven for about 10 minutes. Serve hot, split and spread with butter and honey or cold spread with butter or clotted cream.

26   SAVOURY SCONES

Preparation time:	YOU WILL NEED:
10 minutes	*225 g/8 oz self-raising flour*
	½ teaspoon baking powder
Cooking time:	*pinch of salt*
10 minutes	*1 teaspoon dry mustard*
	50 g/2 oz butter or margarine
Oven temperature:	*75 g/3 oz Cheddar cheese, grated*
220C/425F/gas 7	*50 g/2 oz cooked sliced ham, diced*
	about 150 ml/¼ pint milk
Makes about 12	*milk, to glaze*

Calories:
130 per portion

Sift the flour, baking powder, salt and mustard into a bowl. Rub in the butter until the mixture resembles fine breadcrumbs. Stir in the cheese and ham and enough milk to mix to a soft dough.

Turn on to a floured surface, knead lightly and roll out to 2 cm/¾ inch thickness. Cut into 5 cm/2 inch rounds and place on a lightly floured baking tray. Brush with milk to glaze.

Bake for 10 minutes, then cool on a wire rack. Serve with butter.

▪ COOK'S TIP

These delicious scones can also be cooked on a lightly greased griddle, turning them over when the bases are golden brown.

▪ COOK'S TIP

Brown scones, rather like brown bread, are becoming more favoured for good health. The above recipe can also be made with wholemeal flour but *substitute only half of the flour. Serve with soups, salads and other cold fare.*

27 COTSWOLD SCONE RING

Preparation time:
10-15 minutes

Cooking time:
15-20 minutes

Oven temperature:
220C/425F/gas 7

Makes 8

Calories:
285 per portion

YOU WILL NEED:
225 g/8 oz self-raising flour
1 teaspoon baking powder
pinch of salt
1 teaspoon dry mustard
40 g/1½ oz butter or margarine
100 g/4 oz Cotswold cheese with
    chives, grated
about 150 ml/¼ pint milk
beaten egg, to glaze
FOR THE FILLING
2 x 62.5 g/2.2 oz packets soft
    cream cheese
2 tablespoons snipped chives
½ teaspoon garlic granules

Sift the flour, baking powder, salt and mustard into a bowl. Rub in the butter until the mixture resembles fine breadcrumbs. Stir in the cheese and add enough milk to mix to a soft dough.

Turn on to a floured surface and knead until smooth. Roll out to a 1 cm/½ inch thickness. Using a 7.5 cm/3 inch plain cutter, cut out eight scones. Arrange them in a circle, overlapping slightly, on a greased baking tray. Brush with egg to glaze. Bake for 15-20 minutes, or until firm and golden. Cool on a wire rack.

To make the filling, mix the cream cheese with the chives and garlic granules. Break the scones apart while still warm, split each one and spread with the cheese mixture. Serve immediately.

28 BASIC SCONES

Preparation time:
10-15 minutes

Cooking time:
10 minutes

Oven temperature:
220C/425F/gas 7

Makes about 10

Calories:
136 per portion

YOU WILL NEED:
225 g/8 oz plain flour
1 teaspoon cream of tartar
½ teaspoon bicarbonate of soda
pinch of salt
50 g/2 oz butter or margarine
25 g/1 oz caster sugar
about 6 tablespoons milk
milk, to glaze

Sift the flour, cream of tartar, bicarbonate of soda and salt into a bowl. Rub in the butter until the mixture resembles fine breadcrumbs. Stir in the sugar and enough milk to mix to a soft dough.

Turn on to a floured surface, knead lightly and roll out to a 2 cm/¾ inch thickness. Cut into 5 cm/2 inch rounds and place on a floured baking tray. Brush with milk to glaze.

Bake for 10 minutes, then transfer to a wire rack to cool. Serve with butter or cream, and jam.

■ COOK'S TIP

These savoury scones are a boon for packed lunches, picnics or buffet lunches. Vary the topping occasionally by sprinkling with grated cheese, poppyseeds, sesame seeds or coarse sea salt instead of the plain egg glaze.

■ COOK'S TIP

Wholemeal scones can be made using the above method and ingredients; simply substitute 100 g/4 oz plain wholemeal flour for 100 g/4 oz plain white flour.

29 DROP SCONES

Preparation time:	YOU WILL NEED:
5 minutes	*225 g/8 oz self-raising flour*
	2 teaspoons baking powder
Cooking time:	*pinch of salt*
about 4 minutes	*25 g/1 oz caster sugar*
	1 egg
Makes about 25	*300 ml/½ pint milk*

Calories:
46 per portion

Sift the flour, baking powder and salt into a bowl. Stir in the sugar. Make a well in the centre of the flour and drop in the egg. Beat in the milk gradually to form a fairly thick batter.

Grease a griddle or heavy-based frying pan lightly. Place over a moderate heat. Drop tablespoonsful of the batter on to the pan, a little distance apart and cook until bubbles appear on the surface of the scones. Turn and cook on the other side for about 1 minute.

Keep the scones warm while cooking the remaining batter. Serve warm, with butter and preserves.

◼ COOK'S TIP

Cover cooked scones with a clean teatowel to prevent them drying out while you cook the remaining batter.

30 SALLY LUNNS

Preparation time:	YOU WILL NEED:
25 minutes, plus rising	*450 g/1 lb strong white flour*
	1 teaspoon salt
Cooking time:	*15 g/½ oz fresh yeast or 1½*
25 minutes	*teaspoons dried yeast*
	1 teaspoon granulated sugar
Oven temperature:	*50 ml/2 fl oz warm water*
220C/425F/gas 7	*150 ml/¼ pint single cream or milk*
	50 g/2 oz butter
Makes 2 x15 cm/6	*2 eggs, beaten*
inch round cakes	*Sweet milk glaze (see Cook's Tip)*

Calories:
1258 per cake

Sift the flour and salt into a warm bowl. Dissolve the yeast with the sugar in the water and leave to froth. Warm the cream or milk, dissolve the butter in it and cool slightly. Mix in the beaten eggs and add to the yeast. Make a well in the flour and stir in the liquid. Mix to a smooth soft dough. Cover and leave in a warm place until doubled in bulk.

Turn on to a floured board and knead carefully. Grease and warm two 15 cm/6 inch round cake tins. Divide the dough in half and mould each half into a ball. Put a ball into each tin, cover and leave until it has risen again and fills the tins.

Bake in the centre of the oven for 20 minutes or until a skewer inserted comes out clean. Bring the hot glaze to the boil and brush over the cakes while still in the tin. Allow to shrink before turning out. Cut horizontally into two or three rounds and spread with butter or clotted cream. Reassemble the cakes.

◼ COOK'S TIP

For Sweet milk glaze, dissolve 2 tablespoons sugar in 2 tablespoons hot milk and brush over the Sally Lunns.

31 PENNY BUNS

Preparation time:
30 minutes, plus rising

Cooking time:
about 15 minutes

Oven temperature:
220C/425F/gas 7

Makes about 16

Calories:
209 per portion

YOU WILL NEED:
575 g/1¼ lb strong white flour
15 g/½ oz fresh yeast
1 teaspoon granulated sugar
about 600 ml/1 pint warm milk
50 g/2 oz butter, cut up
1 egg, beaten
75 g/3 oz currants
50 g/2 oz caster sugar
Sweet milk glaze (see recipe 27),
    to coat

Stir half the flour into a warm bowl. Blend the yeast with the granulated sugar, and add 150 ml/¼ pint of the warm milk. Mix into a firm dough, adding a little more milk if necessary. Beat well. Cover and leave to rise for 30-40 minutes.

Dissolve the butter in the remaining milk, pour into the beaten egg and stir well. Mix the liquid into the risen dough with the remaining flour, the currants and caster sugar. Beat well and leave in a warm place until doubled in bulk. Knead lightly and scoop off pieces of dough weighing about 50 g/2 oz each. Shape each piece into a smooth ball, place on a greased baking tray and flatten slightly. Cover and prove until springy to the touch. Bake for about 15 minutes. Remove and brush with the glaze, then replace in the oven briefly for the glaze to dry. Cool on a wire rack.

32 SINGIN' HINNY

Preparation time:
10 minutes

Cooking time:
20 minutes

Makes 8 wedges

Calories:
231 per portion

YOU WILL NEED:
225 g/8 oz self-raising flour
½ teaspoon salt
50 g/2 oz lard
50 g/2 oz caster sugar
75 g/3 oz currants
1 egg, beaten
6 tablespoons milk

Place the flour and salt in a bowl. Add the lard, cut into pieces and rub into the flour until the mixture resembles fine breadcrumbs. Stir in the sugar and currants. Add the beaten egg and milk and mix to a soft dough.

Turn out on to a lightly floured surface and knead lightly. Roll or press out to a 20 cm/8 inch round.

Heat a griddle or heavy-based frying pan, which has been lightly greased with oil. Cook the cake over a low heat for 10 minutes, then turn it over carefully and cook for a further 10 minutes.

Slide the cake on to a plate and cut into eight wedges. Serve warm, split and buttered.

▪ COOK'S TIP

These buns have retained their original name although they can no longer be bought for a penny! Serve freshly baked, or split, toasted and buttered.

▪ COOK'S TIP

Light handling is the secret to light results when making this griddle cake. Mix just sufficiently to bind the mixture, knead it very briefly and don't worry if there are a few cracks in the dough. It burns easily so keep the heat low.

33 AMERICAN BANANA LOAF

Preparation time:	YOU WILL NEED:
15-20 minutes	225 g/8 oz plain flour
	1 teaspoon bicarbonate of soda
Cooking time:	½ teaspoon cream of tartar
about 1¼ hours	pinch of salt
	100 g/4 oz butter or margarine
Oven temperature:	175 g/6 oz caster sugar
180C/350F/gas 4	1 teaspoon lemon juice
	3 tablespoons milk
Makes 1 x 23 x 13	2 bananas, mashed
cm/9 x 5 inch loaf	1 teaspoon grated lemon rind
	2 eggs, beaten
Total calories:	granulated sugar, to dredge
2640	

Sift the flour, bicarbonate of soda, cream of tartar and salt into a mixing bowl. Rub the fat in until the mixture resembles fine breadcrumbs. Mix in the sugar thoroughly. Add the lemon juice to the milk. Mix the mashed banana with the lemon rind in a small bowl. Stir in the curdled milk and beaten eggs. Make a well in the flour and mix in the banana mixture.

Turn into a greased and base-lined 23 x 13 cm/9 x 5 inch loaf tin, smooth the top, and dredge with granulated sugar. Bake in the centre of the oven for 1¼ hours or until a skewer inserted in the centre comes out clean.

34 PANETTONE

Preparation time:	YOU WILL NEED:
30 minutes, plus rising	1 teaspoon granulated sugar
	1 tablespoon dried yeast
Cooking time:	4 tablespoons warm milk
40 minutes	100 g/4 oz butter
	50 g/2 oz caster sugar
Oven temperature:	3 eggs, beaten
200C/400F/gas 6;	grated rind of ½ lemon
180C/350F/gas 4	400 g/14 oz white bread flour
	1 teaspoon salt
Serves 8-10	100 g/4 oz raisins
	75 g/3 oz cut mixed peel
Calories:	beaten egg, to glaze
403-322	

Sprinkle the granulated sugar and yeast over the warm milk in a small bowl. Leave until frothy, about 10 minutes. Beat together the butter and caster sugar until light and fluffy, about 5 minutes. Beat in the eggs, a little at a time, then beat in the lemon rind. Place the flour and salt in a large bowl. Stir in the yeast liquid and creamed mixture, and mix until a soft dough is formed. Place the dough on a floured surface and knead until smooth, silky and no longer sticky. Place in an oiled polythene bag and leave to rise until doubled in size, about 1 hour.

Sprinkle the raisins and peel over the dough and knead until thoroughly mixed in. Place in a greased 20 cm/8 inch cake tin and leave until doubled in size, about 45 minutes.

Brush the dough with the beaten egg and bake at the higher temperature for 10 minutes, then at the lower for 30 minutes until deep golden brown and firm to the touch.

■ COOK'S TIP

When moistened, bicarbonate of soda soon produces the bubbles that make mixtures rise. Therefore it is important that such items are put in the oven as soon as they are mixed.

■ COOK'S TIP

Panettone will keep well for up to a week wrapped in foil and stored in a container that is not airtight. If it gets a little dry, it is delicious toasted.

35 BANANA RAISIN BREAD

Preparation time: 15 minutes	YOU WILL NEED: 225 g/8 oz self-raising flour
	½ teaspoon salt
Cooking time: 1½ hours	100 g/4 oz butter or margarine
	175 g/6 oz dark brown sugar
	75 g/3 oz raisins
Oven temperature: 160C/325F/gas 3	2 ripe bananas
	½ teaspoon vanilla essence
	1 egg, beaten
Makes 1 x 1 kg/2 lb loaf	3 tablespoons milk
Total calories: 2760	

Put the flour and salt in a bowl. Add the butter or margarine, cut into pieces, and rub into the flour until the mixture resembles fine breadcrumbs. Stir in the sugar and raisins. Mash the bananas with a fork and add to the mixture with the vanilla essence, beaten egg and milk. Beat until well mixed.

Turn the mixture into a greased and base-lined 1 kg/2 lb loaf tin and smooth the top with the back of a spoon. Place the tin on a baking tray and bake for 1½ hours, until the cake is golden brown and springs back when pressed with the fingers.

Leave in the tin for 10 minutes, then turn out and cool on a wire rack. Serve sliced and buttered.

36 DATE AND LEMON LOAF

Preparation time: 15 minutes	YOU WILL NEED: 225 g/8 oz stoneless dates, chopped
	175 g/6 oz margarine
Cooking time: 45 minutes	175 g/6 oz soft dark brown sugar
	75 g/3 oz golden syrup
	grated rind of 1 lemon
Oven temperature: 160C/325F/gas 3	3 eggs, beaten
	275 g/10 oz self-raising flour
	½ teaspoon salt
Makes 1 x 1.5 kg/3 lb loaf	FOR THE TOPPING
	2 tablespoons plain flour
	1 tablespoon demerara sugar
Total calories: 4145	15 g/½ oz butter

Place the dates, margarine, sugar and syrup in a large saucepan. Heat gently until the margarine has melted and the sugar has dissolved. Remove from the heat, allow to cool slightly, then stir in the lemon rind and beaten eggs. Stir in the flour and salt and mix thoroughly and place the mixture in a greased and base-lined 1.5 kg/3 lb loaf tin.

To make the topping, mix together the flour and sugar, then rub in the butter to form a crumble. Sprinkle the crumble evenly over the loaf.

Bake for 45 minutes, until the cake is golden brown and springs back when pressed with the fingers.

Leave the loaf to cool in the tin for 15 minutes, then turn out and leave to cool completely on a wire rack.

■ COOK'S TIP

Try to buy natural brown sugars for baking: that is, those that state the country of origin on the packet. The flavour is better and the sugar remains moister.

■ COOK'S TIP

To make a date and walnut loaf, substitute 50 g/2 oz walnuts, finely chopped, for 50 g/2 oz of the dates.

37 WELSH CAKES

Preparation time:	YOU WILL NEED:
15 minutes	225 g/8 oz plain flour
	1 teaspoon baking powder
Cooking time:	¼ teaspoon mixed spice
8 minutes	50 g/2 oz butter or margarine
	50 g/2 oz lard
Makes about 10	75 g/3 oz caster sugar
	50 g/2 oz currants
Calories:	1 egg, beaten
228 per portion	2-3 tablespoons milk

Sift the flour, baking powder and spice into a mixing bowl. Cut the fats into the flour and rub in until the mixture resembles fine breadcrumbs, then mix in the sugar and currants. Mix in the egg and sufficient milk to make a stiff dough.

Roll out on a floured board to 5 mm/¼ inch thickness. Cut into 7.5 cm/3 inch rounds.

Bake on a hot greased griddle until golden brown, about 4 minutes on each side. Serve hot with butter, sprinkled with cinnamon sugar, or cold spread with honey or jam.

38 PIKELETS

Preparation time:	YOU WILL NEED:
15-20 minutes, plus resting	225 g/8 oz plain or unbleached flour
	1 teaspoon salt
	15 g/½ oz fresh yeast or 1½
Cooking time:	teaspoons dried yeast
about 8 minutes	1 teaspoon granulated sugar
	150 ml/¼ pint warm water
Makes about 20	1 teaspoon butter
	150 ml/¼ pint warm milk
Calories:	1 egg, beaten
54 per portion	

Sift the flour and salt into a warm bowl. Dissolve the yeast and the sugar in the warm water. Melt the butter in the warm milk and beat in the egg. Stir the yeast liquid and then the milk mixture into the flour. Mix in to a smooth batter and beat well. Cover and leave in a warm place for 1 - 1½ hours until the batter is thick and bubbling.

Warm the griddle and grease with a piece of lard on a fork. When a drop of water splutters on the griddle, it is hot enough. Stir the batter and pour it on to the griddle in round 'puddles', leaving space in between so they are easy to turn; yeast batter does not spread as much as pancake batter.

Cook over moderate heat until bubbles break the top surface and the underneath is pale gold. Using a palette knife, flip the pikelets over and cook the other side. Keep each batch warm in a folded cloth in a low oven. Serve hot with butter, honey or preserves.

■ COOK'S TIP

Try these griddle cakes for a picnic lunch, partnered by a chunk of Caerphilly cheese, as eaten by shepherds in the Welsh mountains.

■ COOK'S TIP

Pikelets are also excellent served with cream cheese, grilled bacon or cocktail sausages. To reheat, crisp under the grill.

39 RAISIN, ALMOND AND GRAPEFRUIT LOAF

Preparation time:
20 minutes

Cooking time:
1 hour

Oven temperature:
180C/350F/gas 4

Makes 1 x 1 kg/2 lb loaf

Total calories:
3772

YOU WILL NEED:
450 g/1 lb raisins, coarsely chopped
5 tablespoons water
350 g/12 oz self-raising flour
teaspoon baking powder
50 g/2 oz butter
50 g/2 oz caster sugar
100 g/4 oz blanched almonds,
    coarsely chopped
3 tablespoons milk
5 tablespoons grapefruit juice
2 eggs, beaten
1 grapefruit

Place the raisins in a saucepan with the water and bring slowly to the boil. Remove from the heat.

Sift the flour with the baking powder into a bowl. Rub in the butter, then stir in the sugar and almonds. Add the milk, grapefruit juice, eggs and raisin mixture, and mix well.

Grate the rind from the grapefruit and remove the segments of flesh. Fold the rind and flesh into the cake mixture. Pour into a greased 1 kg/2 lb loaf tin.

Bake for 1 hour or until golden brown. Turn out to cool on a wire rack.

40 FARMHOUSE LOAF

Preparation time:
15 minutes

Cooking time:
50-60 minutes

Oven temperature:
180C/350F/gas 4

Makes one 450 g/1 lb loaf

Total calories:
2351

YOU WILL NEED:
100 g/4 oz self-raising flour
100 g/4 oz plain wholemeal flour
pinch of grated nutmeg
½ teaspoon bicarbonate of soda
75 g/3 oz butter or margarine
100 g/4 oz caster sugar
50 g/2 oz raisins
25 g/1 oz glacé cherries
25 g/1 oz sultanas
25 g/1 oz chopped mixed peel
grated rind of 1 lemon
1 egg, beaten
6 tablespoons milk

Place the flours, nutmeg and bicarbonate of soda in a mixing bowl and rub in the butter or margarine. Add the sugar, fruits, peel and lemon rind. Mix in the egg and milk to produce a mixture with a soft dropping consistency. Spoon into a greased and lined 450 g/1 lb loaf tin.

Bake for 50-60 minutes. Turn out to cool on a wire rack. Serve sliced and spread with butter.

◾ COOK'S TIP

To ensure that you get all the grated grapefruit rind for the cake, brush the pieces of grated rind from the grater with a dry pastry brush.

◾ COOK'S TIP

A soft dropping consistency is achieved when a spoonful of mixture, when raised up from the bowl, drops slowly and easily from the spoon.

41 SPICED COFFEE TEABREAD

Preparation time:	YOU WILL NEED:
15 minutes	225 g/8oz self-raising flour
	100 g/4 oz butter or margarine
Cooking time:	100 g/4 oz soft dark brown sugar
1-1¼ hours	3 tablespoons black coffee
	75 g/3 oz walnuts, chopped
Oven temperature:	2 eggs
180C/350F/gas 4	100 g/4 oz glacé cherries, chopped
	½ teaspoon ground cinnamon
Makes 1 x 1 kg/2 lb	¼ teaspoon ground mixed spice
loaf	grated rind of 1 lemon
Total calories:	
2933	

Place the flour in a mixing bowl and rub in the butter. Stir in the sugar, coffee, walnut, eggs, cherries, cinnamon, mixed spice and lemon rind, and mix well. Spoon into a greased and base-lined 1 kg/2 lb loaf tin.

Bake for 1-1¼ hours, then turn out to cool on a wire rack. Serve sliced and spread with butter.

42 DATE AND PINEAPPLE LOAF

Preparation time:	YOU WILL NEED:
15-20 minutes	50 g/2 oz butter or margarine
	225 g/8 oz stoned dates, chopped
Cooking time:	50 g/2 oz soft light brown sugar
1¼-1½ hours	150 ml/¼ pint water
	1 teaspoon bicarbonate of soda
Oven temperature:	50 g/2 oz glacé pineapple, chopped
160C/325F/gas 3	1 egg, beaten
	225 g/8 oz self-raising flour
Makes 1 x 1 kg/2 lb	FOR THE TOPPING
loaf	2 tablespoons honey
	25 g/1 oz glacé pineapple,
Total calories:	chopped
2447	

Place the butter or margarine, dates, sugar and water in a saucepan and bring to the boil. Remove from the heat and allow to cool.

Add the remaining ingredients and mix well together. Place in a greased and lined 1 kg/2 lb loaf tin. Bake for 1¼-1½ hours, then turn out to cool on a wire rack.

To make the topping, melt the honey and brush over the top of the loaf. Sprinkle with the chopped glacé pineapple and decorate.

▪ COOK'S TIP

When rubbing in the flour and butter, allow only the tips of the fingers and thumbs (the coolest and driest parts) to come in contact with the mixture.

Lift the mixture high from the bowl to trap plenty of air.

▪ COOK'S TIP

If glacé pineapple is not available, then crystallized ginger may be used instead.

43   YORKSHIRE PARKIN

Preparation time:	YOU WILL NEED:
15 minutes	225 g/8 oz plain flour
	½ teaspoon salt
Cooking time:	1 teaspoon ground mixed spice
1 hour	1 teaspoon ground cinnamon
	1 teaspoon ground ginger
Oven temperature:	1 teaspoon bicarbonate of soda
180C/350F/gas 4	225 g/8 oz medium oatmeal
	175 g/6 oz black treacle
Makes 1 x 18 cm/7	150 g/5 oz butter or margarine
inch square cake	100 g/4 oz soft brown sugar
	150 ml/¼ pint milk
Total calories:	1 egg, beaten
3798	

Sift the flour, salt, spices and bicarbonate of soda into a bowl. Mix in the oatmeal.

Place the treacle, butter, sugar and milk in a saucepan and heat gently until well combined and the butter has melted. Add to the dry ingredients and mix well. Stir in the egg, then spoon into a greased and lined 18 cm/7 inch deep, square cake tin.

Bake for 1 hour, then turn out to cool on a wire rack.

Store, wrapped in foil, for about 1 week before cutting into squares to serve.

44   GINGERBREAD RING CAKE

Preparation time:	YOU WILL NEED:
15 minutes	100 g/4 oz butter or margarine
	100 g/4 oz soft brown sugar
Cooking time:	175 g/6 oz black treacle
1-1¼ hours	225 g/8 oz plain flour
	3-4 teaspoons ground ginger
Oven temperature:	½ teaspoon ground cinnamon
160C/325F/gas 3	1 egg, beaten
	½ teaspoon bicarbonate of soda
Makes 1 x 20 cm/8	6 tablespoons milk
inch ring cake	FOR THE ICING AND
	DECORATION
Total calories:	100 g/4 oz icing sugar, sifted
2941	5 teaspoons water
	crystallized ginger

Melt the butter or margarine, sugar and treacle over a low heat until dissolved. Sift the flour and spices into a bowl and pour in the melted mixture and egg. Dissolve the bicarbonate of soda in the milk and stir into the flour mixture, mixing well. Pour quickly into a greased and floured 20 cm/8 inch ring tin.

Bake for 1-¼ hours. Leave in the tin for a few minutes before turning out to cool on a wire rack.

To make the icing, mix the icing sugar with the water until smooth. Pour over the cake, allowing it to run down the sides. Decorate with crystallized ginger.

■ COOK'S TIP

To weigh the treacle without making a mess, first weigh the saucepan that it is to be cooked in, then weigh the treacle in it.

■ COOK'S TIP

This is a good basic recipe that lends itself to variations. For a fruity gingerbread ring add 75 g/3 oz raisins with the dry ingredients. For an orange gingerbread ring add the coarsely grated rind of 2 oranges instead.

45 APRICOT AND WALNUT LOAF

Preparation time:
25 minutes, plus
resting and rising

Cooking time:
45 minutes

Oven temperature:
230C/450F/gas 8;
200C/400F/gas 6

**Makes two small
loaves**

Calories:
1071 per loaf

YOU WILL NEED:
225 g/8 oz wholemeal flour
225 g/8 oz strong white flour
25 g/1 oz granulated sugar
100 g/4 oz dried apricots, snipped
50 g/2 oz walnuts, chopped
15 g/½ oz fresh yeast or 1½
* teaspoons dried yeast with 1*
* teaspoon granulated sugar*
300 ml/½ pint warm milk and water
50 g/2 oz butter, cut up
1 egg, beaten
warm honey, to glaze

Sift the flours into a warm mixing bowl. Mix in the sugar, apricots and walnuts. Dissolve the yeast in half the warm milk and water, adding the sugar if using dried yeast. Leave for 10 minutes or until frothy. Dissolve the butter in the remaining warm milk and water. Stir in the beaten egg. Add all the liquids to the dry ingredients and mix to a smooth dough. Knead, cover and prove in a warm place until doubled in bulk.

Turn on to a floured board, knead lightly and divide in half. Put into two small warmed and greased loaf tins. Cover and prove in a warm place until the dough fills the tins. Bake at the higher temperature for 20 minutes, then at the lower for 15-20 minutes. Brush with warm honey and return to the oven for 4-5 minutes for the glaze to set.

▦ COOK'S TIP

To make a prune and nut loaf, replace the apricots with 100 g/4 oz prunes, chopped, and the walnuts with cashews or almonds. Add 2 teaspoons grated   *orange rind for flavouring.*

46 MANX BUN LOAF

Preparation time:
20 minutes

Cooking time:
1½ hours

Oven temperature:
180C/350F/gas 4

**Makes 1 x 450 g/1 lb
loaf**

Total calories:
3957

YOU WILL NEED:
225 g/8 oz plain flour
pinch of salt
pinch of mixed spice
pinch of ground nutmeg
1 teaspoon bicarbonate of soda
100 g/4 oz lard or butter
100 g/4 oz soft brown sugar
225 g/8 oz sultanas
225 g/8 oz currants
225 g/8 oz raisins
25 g/1 oz chopped mixed peel
1 tablespoon black treacle
250 ml/8 fl oz buttermilk

Sift the flour, salt, mixed spice, nutmeg and bicarbonate of soda into a mixing bowl. Rub the fat until the mixture resembles fine breadcrumbs. Mix in the sugar and dried fruit and peel. Dissolve the treacle in the buttermilk and stir it in. Place the mixture in a greased and base-lined 450 g/1 lb loaf tin and bake for about 1½ hours. A skewer inserted in the centre will come out clean when the loaf is cooked. Allow to shrink slightly before turning out on to a wire rack to cool.

▦ COOK'S TIP

If your local supermarket does not stock buttermilk, use 250 g/8 fl oz milk soured with 2 teaspoons of lemon juice.

47 GLAZED NUT LOAF

Preparation time:
20 minutes

Cooking time:
50-55 minutes

Oven temperature:
180C/350F/gas 4

Makes 1 x 1 kg/2 lb loaf

Total calories:
3106

YOU WILL NEED:
100 g/4 oz butter
100 g/4 oz soft light brown sugar
2 eggs, beaten
100 g/4 oz mixed nuts, finely chopped
8 tablespoons milk
225 g/8 oz self-raising flour
2 teaspoons ground cinnamon
25 g/1 oz whole nuts, to decorate
1 teaspoon warmed honey, to glaze

Place the butter and sugar in a bowl. Beat with a wooden spoon for 10 minutes, or in a mixer for 5 minutes, until light and fluffy. Beat in the eggs, a little at a time. Stir in the nuts and milk. Sift the flour and cinnamon into the bowl, then fold in lightly using a metal spoon.

Turn the mixture into a greased and base-lined 1 kg/2 lb loaf tin and smooth over the top. Arrange a cluster of whole nuts along the centre of the loaf, then place the tin on a baking tray. Bake for 50-55 minutes, until the cake is deep golden brown and springs back when pressed with the fingers. Cool in the tin for 5 minutes, then turn out on to a wire rack. Brush with the warmed honey.

◼ COOK'S TIP

It is important to preheat the oven for at least 15 minutes before baking a cake or loaf (unless your oven manufacturer specifies otherwise).

48 LARDY CAKE

Preparation time:
20-25 minutes, plus rising

Cooking time:
35-40 minutes

Oven temperature:
200C/400F/gas 6

Makes one 25 x 20 cm/10 x 8 inch cake

Total calories:
3032

YOU WILL NEED:
350 g/12 oz strong white flour
1 teaspoon salt
10 g/¼ oz lard
10 g/¼ oz fresh yeast
250 ml/8 fl oz water
100 g/4 oz lard
75 g/3 oz sultanas
25 g/1 oz chopped mixed peel
100 g/4 oz granulated sugar
FOR THE GLAZE
milk
caster sugar

Make the dough according to the recipe for Basic White Bread (recipe 4), leaving to rise until doubled in bulk. Turn on to a floured board and knead lightly. Roll the dough out to about 1 cm/½ inch, then cut a 46 x 18 cm/18 x 7 inch rectangle. Mark across into three sections. Dot the top two-thirds with half the lard and sprinkle with half the fruit, peel and sugar. Fold up the bottom third of the dough, then fold over the top third. Seal the edges with the rolling pin, give a quarter turn and roll out again into a rectangle. Repeat with the remaining lard, fruit and sugar; fold and turn. Roll and fold once again.

Put the dough in a roasting tin lined with foil and greased. Leave in a warm place for 30 minutes or until doubled in bulk. Brush with milk and sprinkle with sugar. Mark into squares with the back of a knife and bake for 35-40 minutes.

◼ COOK'S TIP

You can leave the cake in the tin to soak up any fat which has leaked out or, if you prefer a crisper crust on the base, cool on a wire rack.

SAVOURIES

Not everyone likes eating only sweet foods at teatime, so here is a selection of savouries, from ever-popular potato cakes and Cornish pasties to various kinds of cheese biscuits. There are variations on familiar themes, such as bread pinwheels and sandwiches with fish fillings, and a few unusual ways with cheesecakes, too.

49   MINI PIZZAS

Preparation time:
40 minutes, plus rising

Cooking time:
15-20 minutes per
batch

Oven temperature:
220C/425F/gas 7;
230C/450F/Gas 8

Makes 30

Calories:
103 per portion

YOU WILL NEED:
1 x 500 g/18 oz packet white
    bread mix
3 tablespoons oil
2 onions, finely chopped
2 garlic cloves, crushed
1 x 800 g/28 oz can tomatoes
2 tablespoons tomato purée
2 teaspoons dried mixed herbs
freshly ground black pepper
25 g/1 oz Parmesan cheese, grated
100 g/4 oz cooked ham, chopped
100 g/4 oz salami, chopped
1 x 50 g/2 oz can anchovy fillets,
    drained and chopped
50 g/2 oz black olives, sliced
100 g/4 oz Cheddar cheese, grated

Make up the bread mix and leave to rise.

Heat 2 tablespoons oil in a pan, add the onions and garlic and fry until soft. Add the tomatoes with their juice, the purée, herbs and pepper. Simmer until the mixture thickens.

Roll out the bread dough to 5 mm/¼ inch thickness. Cut into 6 cm/2½ inch circles and place on greased baking trays. Brush each circle with the remaining oil and sprinkle with the Parmesan cheese. Top with the tomato mixture. Bake for 10-15 minutes until risen and golden brown.

Mix the ham, salami and anchovies and divide among the pizzas. Place an olive slice on each and sprinkle with cheese. Return to the oven at the higher temperature for 5 minutes.

▨ COOK'S TIP

It is not necessary to season the tomato mixture with any salt as there is plenty in the other ingredients.

50   BRISLING ENVELOPES

Preparation time:
20 minutes

Cooking time:
30 minutes

Oven temperature:
190C/375F/gas 5

Makes 12

Calories:
189 per portion

YOU WILL NEED:
225 g/8 oz plain flour
salt
100 g/4 oz lard and hard
    margarine, mixed
about 4 tablespoons water
2 x 90 g/3½ oz cans brisling
beaten egg, to glaze
curly endive leaves, to garnish

Sieve the flour and salt into a mixing bowl. Rub in the fat until the mixture resembles fine breadcrumbs. Add sufficient water to form a firm dough.

Turn on to a floured surface and roll out to a rectangular shape. Cut into 12 x 5 cm/2 in squares. Lay the brisling diagonally across the squares and dampen the edges with beaten egg. Fold the 4 corners of each square of pastry over to meet in the middle like an envelope. Brush with beaten egg and place on a greased baking tray.

Bake for 30 minutes until golden brown. Serve warm, garnished with curly endive leaves.

▨ COOK'S TIP

Cans of brisling - which are small sprats - are useful store cupboard items. The fish can be passed through a sieve and used as a sandwich spread.

51 FINGER ROLLS WITH SAVOURY TOPPINGS

Preparation time:
25 minutes

Makes 24

Calories:
120 per portion

YOU WILL NEED:
12 finger rolls, halved
75 g/3 oz butter, softened
CREAM CHEESE AND PINEAPPLE
TOPPING
225 g/8 oz full-fat soft cheese
1 x 215 g/7½ oz can crushed
    pineapple, drained
1 tablespoon mayonnaise
TUNA FISH AND MAYONNAISE
TOPPING
1 x 200 g/7 oz can tuna in oil,
    drained and flaked
3 tablespoons mayonnaise
2 teaspoons lemon juice
salt and pepper
FOR THE GARNISH
stuffed olives, sliced
lemon slices, quartered
cucumber slices, quartered
thin slices of radish

Cut the finger rolls in half lengthwise and spread thinly with butter.

Mix together the ingredients for the chosen topping and spread on the rolls. Serve garnished with olive, lemon, cucumber and radish slices.

COOK'S TIP

If kept in the refrigerator and covered with cling film, the garnish items can be prepared earlier in the day and arranged on the rolls just before serving.

52 CHEESE AND ANCHOVY TWISTS

Preparation time:
about 15 minutes

Cooking time:
about 15 minutes

Oven temperature:
220C/425F/gas 7

Makes about 50

Calories:
12 per portion

YOU WILL NEED:
100 g/4 oz puff or shortcrust pastry
2 x 40 g/1½ oz cans anchovy
    fillets (See Cook's Tip)
a little milk
2 tablespoons grated Parmesan cheese

Roll out the pastry to a 30 cm/12 inch square about 3 mm/⅛ inch thick. Trim the edges neatly with a sharp knife. Cut the pastry into quarters, then cut each quarter into strips 1-2 cm/½-¼ inch wide.

Cut the anchovy fillets in half lengthways. Brush the pastry strips with milk, then lay a piece of anchovy on each one. Sprinkle with the Parmesan cheese.

Give each strip one or two twists and lay on a baking tray lined with non-stick parchment. Bake for about 15 minutes or until lightly browned. Transfer to a wire rack and leave to cool completely, then store in an airtight container. Serve warm or cold.

COOK'S TIP

Put the anchovy fillets in a dish and cover with milk. Leave for at least 5 minutes and then drain well. The longer the anchovies soak, the less salty they will be.

53 CHEESE D'ARTOIS

Preparation time:	YOU WILL NEED:
20 minutes	50 g/2 oz butter
	2 eggs
Cooking time:	100 g/4 oz Cheddar cheese, grated
20 minutes	1 teaspoon paprika
	salt and pepper
Oven temperature:	225 g/8 oz rough puff or flaky pastry
230C/450F/gas 8	100 g/4 oz sliced continental smoked
	sausage, skinned and diced
Makes 12	1 egg yolk beaten with 1 tablespoon
	water, to glaze
Calories:	
213 per portion	

Melt the butter and leave to cool, but not harden. Beat the eggs in a bowl with a fork and mix in the butter, grated cheese and paprika. Add salt and pepper.

Divide the pastry dough in half and roll out each half thinly into a rectangle 15 x 20 cm/6 x 8 inches. Place one half on a baking tray and mark it lightly into 5 cm/2 inch squares. Put some smoked sausage in each square and cover with the cheese mixture. Brush the pastry around the fillings with water, cover with the remaining pastry and mark the top into corresponding squares. Press the damp edges firmly together.

Brush all over with the beaten egg yolk and water. Cut 2 or 3 slits in the top of each square. Bake for 20 minutes or until golden brown. Remove from the oven and cut into squares.

54 CORNISH PASTIES

Preparation time:	YOU WILL NEED:
25 minutes	450 g/1 lb topside of beef, minced
	100 g/4 oz cooked potato or
Cooking time:	turnip, diced
about 1 hour	100 g/4 oz onion, finely chopped
	2 tablespoons chopped parsley
Oven temperature:	¼ teaspoon mixed dried herbs
200C/400F/gas 6;	salt and pepper
180C/350F/gas 4	450 g/1 lb shortcrust pastry
	1 egg, beaten
Makes 8	
Calories:	
385 per portion	

Mix the meat with the vegetables, parsley and dried herbs. Season well with salt and pepper. Roll out the pastry to 5 mm/¼ inch thickness and cut into 15 cm/6 inch rounds, using a small plate. The trimmings can be worked up and re-rolled.

Divide the filling between the pastry rounds, placing it in the centre. Brush the edges with water and draw them up to meet on top of the filling. Press firmly together, crimp with a fork and pinch into flutes. Place on a greased baking tray and brush all over with beaten egg. Roll some pastry scraps into a thick 'cord', shape into initials and press on the side of the pasties. Brush with beaten egg and cut 2 slits in each side.

Bake at the higher temperature for 15 minutes, then lower the heat and cook for a further 35-50 minutes or until golden. Serve hot or allow to cool and store in an airtight container.

■ COOK'S TIP

These can also be served as cocktail savouries. Line small patty tins with pastry, prick the base and three-quarters fill with the cheese mixture. Bake as above for 15 minutes or until well risen and golden.

■ COOK'S TIP

If using chopped cooked meat left over from a roast, the filling should be moistened with gravy and the pastry baked for not more than 25-30 minutes.

55 POTATO CAKES

Preparation time:
20 minutes

Cooking time:
10 minutes

Makes 8-10

Calories:
170-136 per portion

YOU WILL NEED:
450 g/1 lb cooked floury potatoes.
1 teaspoon salt
50 g/2 oz butter, softened
about 4 tablespoons self-raising flour
butter, for filling

Drain the cooked potatoes thoroughly and cover with a clean teatowel until dry and floury. Then sieve into a mixing bowl with the salt. Beat in the butter and work in sufficient flour to make a soft dough which is easy to handle.

Turn on to a floured board and roll or pat out to 2 cm/¾ inch thickness. Cut into rounds with a 7.5 cm/3 inch scone cutter. Place on a hot greased griddle and cook over moderate heat until golden brown underneath. Turn over and cook the other side.

Remove from the griddle, split, butter generously and close together. Keep warm while cooking the next batch. Serve hot.

56 PEANUT SABLES

Preparation time:
25 minutes

Cooking time:
10-15 minutes

Oven temperature:
190C/375F/gas 5

Makes 60

Calories:
54 per portion

YOU WILL NEED:
175 g/6 oz butter
175 g/6 oz plain flour, sifted
175 g/6 oz Cheddar cheese, grated
salt and pepper
1 egg, beaten to glaze
100 g/4 oz salted peanuts, coarsely
   chopped

Rub the fat into the flour until the mixture resembles fine breadcrumbs. Add the cheese and seasoning, and knead together to make a dough.

Roll out the dough thinly and cut into strips 5 cm/2 inches wide. Brush with beaten egg, sprinkle with peanuts and cut each strip into triangles.

Place the triangles on a baking tray lined with greaseproof paper. (Cheese scorches easily, so you can lift the greaseproof paper off the baking tray as soon as the triangles come out of the oven, to prevent further cooking.) Bake for 10-15 minutes until golden brown. Cool on a wire rack. Serve cold.

■ COOK'S TIP

It is easiest to make the potato cakes with hot, freshly cooked potatoes. If using cold potatoes, melt the butter before adding it. Choose a floury potato .

■ COOK'S TIP

The sablés can be frozen for up to 2 months. Pack very carefully in a rigid box, interleaved with plastic tissue or soft paper. Thaw for 1 hour at room temperature. Alternatively, they can be kept in an airtight container for a week.

57 CHEESE AND ALMOND SABLES

Preparation time:	YOU WILL NEED:
20 minutes	*75 g/3 oz plain flour*
	½ teaspoon paprika
Cooking time:	*salt and pepper*
about 10 minutes	*50 g/2 oz butter or lard*
	25 g/1 oz ground almonds
Oven temperature:	*40 g/1½ oz hard cheese, grated*
180C/350F/gas 4	*1 egg yolk*
	FOR THE GLAZE
Makes 24	*1 egg, beaten*
	3-4 tablespoons grated cheese
Calories:	
53 per portion	

Sift the flour, paprika, salt and pepper into a mixing bowl. Cut the fat into the flour and rub in to a breadcrumb consistency. Mix in the almonds and grated cheese. Stir in the egg yolk and mix to a soft dough.

Roll out to 5 mm/¼ inch thickness. Cut out 5 cm/2 inch rounds and place on a greased baking tray. Brush with the beaten egg and sprinkle thickly with the grated cheese.

Bake for 10 minutes or until set and golden brown. Remove from the oven and cool slightly before removing from the baking tray. Serve warm or cold.

58 APPLE AND POTATO CAKE

Preparation time:	YOU WILL NEED:
25 minutes	*675 g/1½ lb cooked floury potatoes*
	3 teaspoons salt
Cooking time:	*50 g/2 oz butter or margarine*
10-15 minutes	*about 4 tablespoons self-raising*
	flour, sifted
Serves 6	*2-3 dessert apples, peeled, cored*
	and chopped
Total calories:	*2 tablespoons caster sugar*
263	*2-3 tablespoons softened butter*

Drain the cooked potatoes thoroughly and cover with a clean teatowel until dry and fluffy, but still very hot. Pass through a wire sieve and weigh off 450 g/1 lb. Put the sieved potato in a warm mixing bowl and beat in the fat. Work in sufficient flour to make the dough manageable, adding salt to taste.

Divide the dough in half and roll out into 2 rounds of equal size just over 1.5 cm/½ inch thick. Place one round on a warmed and greased griddle and spread with the apple. Cover with the other round and pinch the edges together. Bake on the griddle over moderate heat until brown underneath. Slide the greased base of a cake tin underneath, turn the cake over and cook the other side.

Slide the cake on to a hot serving dish, fold back one half of the top, sprinkle the apples with sugar and spread with softened butter. Repeat with the other half of the cake and serve at once dredged with caster sugar.

■ COOK'S TIP

Miniature versions of these delicious savoury biscuits are very popular at drinks parties. Use small decorative cutters in different shapes.

■ COOK'S TIP

If no griddle is available, the cake can be cooked in the oven at 200C/400F, gas 6 for about 30 minutes without turning. If preferred, used Bramley *apples which go fluffy when cooked instead of the dessert apples which keep their shape.*

59   PARMESAN BISCUITS

Preparation time:
20 minutes

Cooking time:
about 10 minutes

Oven temperature:
180C/350F/gas 4

Makes 18-24

Calories:
47-36 per portion

YOU WILL NEED:
50 g/2 oz salted butter
50 g/2 oz plain flour
pinch of cayenne pepper
freshly ground black pepper
50 g/2 oz grated Parmesan cheese

Cream the butter. Season the flour with cayenne and black pepper and gradually work into the butter with the cheese. Knead until smooth and chill for about 30 minutes or until stiffened.

Roll out on a floured board to 5 mm/¼ inch thickness. Cut into small rounds or squares and using a palette knife, place on a greased baking tray. Work up the trimmings, pinch off little pieces and roll into balls. Place on the baking tray and flatten into biscuits. Prick well with a fork.

Bake in a preheated oven for about 10 minutes until set and golden. Cool on a wire rack and store in an airtight container.

60   SMOKED SALMON TRIANGLES

Preparation time:
20 minutes

Makes 64

Calories:
18 per portion

YOU WILL NEED:
8 slices brown bread, crusts
  removed
50 g/2 oz butter, softened
225 g/8 oz smoked salmon, very
  thinly sliced
freshly ground black pepper
lemon juice
1 lemon, cut into wedges

Spread the slices of bread with the butter. Cover each slice neatly with triangular pieces of smoked salmon and sprinkle with pepper and lemon juice.

Cut each slice into 8 triangles. Garnish and serve.

▪ COOK'S TIP

Buy a piece of Parmesan cheese and grate it as you need it. Cartons of ready-grated cheese do not taste as good.

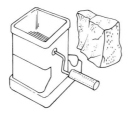

▪ COOK'S TIP

The triangles can be made the day before, covered with cling film and kept in the refrigerator. They can also be frozen for up to 1 month and thawed for 40   *minutes at room temperature.*

61 CHEESE WHIRLS

Preparation time:
20 minutes

Cooking time:
15 minutes

Oven temperature:
220C/425F/gas 7

Makes 20

Calories:
93 per portion

YOU WILL NEED:
225 g/8 oz frozen puff pastry, thawed
3 teaspoons yeast extract
225 g/8 oz Cheddar cheese, finely
*   grated*

Roll the pastry out thinly to a 30 cm/12 inch square. Dot liberally with the yeast extract. Sprinkle with the cheese, reserving 3-4 tablespoons for the topping.

Roll up the pastry carefully to make a Swiss roll shape. Using a sharp knife, cut into 20 thin slices. Arrange the slices flat on a dampened baking sheet, adjusting the round shape as necessary. Sprinkle the remaining cheese on top of each whirl.

Bake for 15 minutes. Transfer to a wire rack immediately. Serve hot or cold.

62 SMOKED COD'S ROE PINWHEELS

Preparation time:
about 25 minutes,
plus chilling

Makes 40

Calories:
45 per portion

YOU WILL NEED:
100 g/4 oz smoked cod's roe
1-2 teaspoons lemon juice
100 g/4 oz softened butter
freshly ground black pepper
1 tablespoon chopped parsley
*   (optional)*
1 small uncut brown loaf, crusts
*   removed*
parsley sprigs, to garnish

Mash the cod's roe with the lemon juice with a fork in a bowl, then beat in the butter until smooth. Season to taste with pepper and stir in the parsley, if using.

Cut the loaf lengthways into 4 thin slices. Spread the bread slices with the smoked cod's roe mixture and roll up neatly beginning with a short end. Wrap the rolls tightly in cling film or non-stick parchment, screwing the ends together, and chill for at least 1 hour or overnight.

Cut the rolls crossways into thin slices and arrange on a plate. Garnish with parsley strips.

■ COOK'S TIP

Try spreading garlic purée very lightly over the pastry instead of using yeast extract. The purée is sold in tubes in large supermarkets.

■ COOK'S TIP

Other savoury mixtures can be used to fill the pinwheel sandwiches, such as canned dressed crab, smooth pâté mixed with softened butter or sieved hard-boiled egg *mixed with a little curry-flavoured mayonnaise.*

63 SCRAMBLED EGG AND CHIVE ON FRIED CROUTES

Preparation time:
20 minutes

Cooking time:
4-5 minutes

Makes 12

Calories:
119 per portion

YOU WILL NEED:
4 eggs
salt and pepper
40 g/1½ oz butter
4 tablespoons mayonnaise
2 tablespoons finely snipped chives
FOR THE CROUTES
6 slices of bread
oil for deep frying
FOR THE GARNISH
12 small green grapes
12 small black grapes

To make the croûtes, remove the crusts from the bread and cut into 5 cm/2 inch squares, using a very sharp knife. Heat the oil to 180-190C/350-375F or until a cube of bread browns in 30 seconds. Lower the bread squares into the oil and toss them frequently until golden brown. Lift out on to absorbent kitchen paper to drain and leave to cool.

Beat the eggs in a bowl with salt and pepper. Melt the butter in a pan and add the beaten egg. Cook, stirring, over a low heat until the mixture is light and fluffy.

Leave to cool, then stir in the mayonnaise and chives. Top each croûte with a little of the scrambled egg mixture and garnish with the green and black grapes.

64 OVEN-BAKED HOTDOGS

Preparation time:
15 minutes

Cooking time:
20 minutes

Oven temperature:
200C/400F/gas 6

Makes 12

Calories:
194 per portion

YOU WILL NEED:
12 thin slices white bread
75 g/3 oz soft margarine
ready-made mustard
12 rashers of streaky bacon, rinds removed
12 skinless sausages

Cut the crusts from each slice of bread and roll out the slices with a rolling pin until thin and even. Spread one side of the bread with margarine and a little mustard. Stretch the bacon rashers with a palette knife until thin and lay one on each slice of bread. Put a sausage at one end of each slice of bread, then roll up firmly like a Swiss roll, securing with a wooden cocktail stick.

Spread a little more margarine on the top of each roll and place on a baking tray. Bake for 20 minutes until golden brown. Serve warm with mustard on one side.

▪ COOK'S TIP

The croûtes are very crunchy so make an excellent base for many creamy savoury mixtures. If packed in an airtight container, they will keep for 3 months in the freezer.

▪ COOK'S TIP

These hot dogs make a very substantial snack. You can vary the fillings; children love tomato ketchup as a substitute for the mustard, or horseradish sauce.

65　CUCUMBER CHEESECAKE

Preparation time:	YOU WILL NEED:
30 minutes, plus	*75 g/3 oz butter, melted*
chilling	*175 g/6 oz water biscuits, crushed*
	grated rind of ½ lemon
Serves 6-8	*1 tablespoon lemon juice*
	salt and pepper
Calories:	*½ large cucumber, grated*
454-340 per portion	*15 g/½ oz sachet powdered gelatine*
	3 tablespoons water
	225 g/8 oz full fat soft cheese
	2 eggs, separated
	grated rind of ½ lemon
	1 tablespoon chopped fresh mint
	*　or 1 teaspoon dried mint*
	150 ml/¼ pint soured cream
	1 garlic clove, crushed

Mix the butter, biscuits, lemon rind and juice. Season to taste. Press evenly into a greased loose-bottomed 18-20 cm/7-8 inch cake tin. Chill while making the filling.

Wrap the grated cucumber in a piece of muslin and squeeze to drain. Sprinkle the gelatine over the water in a bowl and leave for 2-3 minutes until spongy. Stand the bowl in a pan of hot water and stir until the mixture has dissolved. Set aside.

Beat the cheese in a bowl. Beat in the egg yolks, lemon rind, mint, soured cream and garlic. Stir in the gelatine and cucumber. Season. Leave until the mixture is on the point of setting. Whisk the egg whites until stiff. Fold into the cheese mixture. Turn the mixture into the prepared tin. Chill for 3-4 hours, until set. Garnish with cucumber and mint, if liked.

■ COOK'S TIP

The cucumber slices look even more decorative if you use a canelle knife to cut away narrow strips of skin before slicing the cucumber.

66　AVOCADO CHEESECAKE

Preparation time:	YOU WILL NEED:
30 minutes, plus	*75 g/3 oz butter, melted*
chilling	*175 g/6 oz Melba toast, crushed*
	grated rind of ½ lemon
Serves 6-8	*salt and pepper*
	FOR THE FILLING
Calories:	*15 g/½ oz sachet powdered gelatine*
573-430 per portion	*3 tablespoons water*
	1 large avocado, halved and stoned
	grated rind of ½ lemon
	1 tablespoon lemon juice
	225 g/8 oz herb-flavoured full-fat
	*　soft cheese*
	2 eggs, separated
	150 ml/¼ pint soured cream
	avocado slices
	2 tablespoons lemon juice

Mix the butter, toast crumbs and lemon rind. Season. Press evenly into a greased loose-bottomed 18-20 cm/7-8 inch cake tin. Chill while making the filling.

Prepare the gelatine as for Cucumber cheesecake (recipe 65). Mash the avocado flesh with the lemon rind and juice until smooth. Beat the cheese in a bowl until softened. Beat in the egg yolks, soured cream and avocado purée. Stir in the gelatine and seasoning. Leave until on the point of setting.

Whisk the egg whites until stiff. Fold lightly but thoroughly into the cheese mixture. Turn into the prepared tin. Chill for 3-4 hours, until set. Transfer to a plate. Turn the avocado slices in the lemon juice and arrange on top of the cheesecake.

■ COOK'S TIP

Do not worry if you find the avocado flesh is streaked with brown when you cut it open. This has happened because the avocados were stored at too *low a temperature. The taste will not be affected.*

67 NEAPOLITAN CHEESECAKE

Preparation time:
30 minutes, plus
chilling

Serves 6-8

Calories:
563-423 per portion

YOU WILL NEED:
75 g/3 oz butter, melted
175 g/6 oz digestive biscuits, crushed
25 g/1 oz grated Parmesan cheese
salt and pepper
FOR THE FILLING
15 g/½ oz sachet powdered gelatine
3 tablespoons water
225 g/8 oz full-fat soft cheese
1 tablespoon tomato purée
½ teaspoon caster sugar
2 eggs, separated
1 small onion, grated
150 ml/¼ pint double cream
1 tablespoon chopped fresh basil
4 large tomatoes, skinned, seeded
and chopped

Mix the butter, biscuit crumbs and grated cheese. Season to taste. Press evenly into a greased loose-bottomed 18-20 cm/7-8 inch cake tin and chill while making the filling.

Prepare the gelatine as for Cucumber cheesecake (recipe 65) Beat the cheese until softened. Beat in the tomato purée, sugar, egg yolks, onion, cream and basil. Stir in the gelatine and season. Leave until the mixture is on the point of setting.

Whisk the egg whites until stiff. Fold lightly, but thoroughly, into the cheese mixture with the chopped tomatoes. Turn the mixture into the prepared tin. Chill for 3-4 hours, until set. Transfer to a plate and garnish with tomatoes and basil, if liked.

▢ COOK'S TIP

Make sure that there is not a spot of grease on the bowl or whisk when whisking egg whites. If doubtful, rub a cut lemon around the inside of the bowl.

68 SUMMER SALAD CHEESECAKE

Preparation time:
30 minutes, plus
chilling

Serves 8-10

Calories:
759-607 per portion

YOU WILL NEED:
100 g/4 oz butter, melted
175 g/6 oz water biscuits, crushed
50 g/2 oz grated Parmesan cheese
salt and pepper
FOR THE FILLING
2 x 15 g/½ oz sachets powdered
gelatine
6 tablespoons water
450 g/1 lb full-fat soft cheese
4 very fresh eggs, separated
75 g/3 oz grated Parmesan cheese
150 ml/¼ pint double cream
150 ml/¼ pint thick mayonnaise
1 large red pepper, chopped
½ small cucumber, thinly sliced
100 g/4 oz cooked ham, diced

Mix the butter, biscuit crumbs and cheese. Season. Press evenly into a greased loose-bottomed 20 cm/8 inch cake tin. Chill.

Sprinkle the gelatine over the water in a heatproof bowl and leave for 2-3 minutes until spongy. Stand the bowl in a pan of hot water and stir until dissolved. Let cool. Beat the soft cheese in a bowl. Beat in the egg yolks, Parmesan, cream and mayonnaise. Stir in the gelatine and season. Leave until about to set. Whisk the egg whites until stiff. Fold into the cheese mixture. Spoon half mixture into the tin. Scatter the red pepper, cucumber and ham over the top. Cover with the remaining cheese mixture and smooth the surface. Chill for 3-4 hours until set. Garnish with pepper rings, if liked

▢ COOK'S TIP

If cucumbers are chilled, you will find they are much easier to slice thinly. Use a very sharp knife or a mandoline.

FAMILY CAKES

The cakes in this chapter are all simple to make and to decorate; they are ideal 'first time' cakes for children and inexperienced bakers to make. There are many long-time family favourites here, including Sticky gingerbread, basic sponges and Chocolate layer cake.

69 ANGEL CAKE

Preparation time:
20 minutes

Cooking time:
1 hour

Oven temperature:
160C/325F/gas 3

**Makes 1 x 18 cm/
7 inch cake**

Total calories:
1146

YOU WILL NEED:
100 g/4 oz plain flour
175 g/6 oz caster sugar
5-6 egg whites
½ teaspoon cream of tartar
½ teaspoon vanilla or almond
  essence

Sift the flour and sugar together three or four times. Beat the egg whites until foamy; add the cream of tartar and whisk until stiff but not dry. Sift the flour and sugar on to the whisked egg whites carefully, about 2 tablespoonfuls at a time, then fold in the flavouring essence.

Turn the mixture into an ungreased 18 cm/7 inch angel cake tin. Bake for 1 hour or until a skewer inserted comes out clean. Remove from the oven and invert on to a wire rack. Leave until quite cold before turning out of the tin.

■ COOK'S TIP

As this is quite a sweet cake, it is best to choose a sharp filling for contrast. Cut the cake across in 3 or down into 8. Spread with lemon curd and reassemble *the cake. Decorate with piped lemon butter cream and crystallized lemon slices. Alternatively, spread with lemon Glacé icing.*

70 BANANA CAKE

Preparation time:
15-20 minutes

Cooking time:
20-25 minutes

Oven temperature:
180C/350F/gas 4

**Makes 1 x 18 cm/
7 inch cake**

Total calories:
2468

YOU WILL NEED:
100 g/4 oz butter or margarine
100 g/4 oz caster sugar
2 eggs
100 g/4 oz self-raising flour, sifted
2 bananas, mashed
icing sugar, to dust
FOR THE FILLING
50 g/2 oz ground almonds
50 g/2 oz icing sugar, sifted
1 small banana, mashed
½ teaspoon lemon juice

Cream the butter or margarine and sugar together until light and fluffy. Add the eggs, one at a time, adding a little flour with the second egg. Fold in the remaining flour with the bananas. Divide the mixture between 2 greased and lined 18 cm/7 inch sandwich tins.

Bake for 20-25 minutes until the cakes spring back when pressed lightly with the fingertips. Turn out to cool on a wire rack.

To make the filling, mix the ground almonds with the icing sugar, then add the banana and lemon juice and mix to a smooth paste. Sandwich the cakes together with the filling and dust with icing sugar.

■ COOK'S TIP

This is the ideal cake to make with those less than perfect or special offer bananas that are just past their peak and are very ripe.

71 APPLE AND CINNAMON CAKE

Preparation time:
15 minutes

Cooking time:
1¼ hours

Oven temperature:
180C/350F/gas 4

**Makes 1 x 20 cm/
8 inch square cake**

Total calories:
3297

YOU WILL NEED:
275 g/10 oz self-raising flour
1½ teaspoons ground cinnamon
225 g/8 oz demerara sugar
50 g/2 oz raisins
100 g/4 oz butter, melted
2 large eggs, beaten
175 ml/6 fl oz milk
225 g/8 oz dessert apples, peeled,
   cored and chopped
icing sugar, to dust

Sift the flour and cinnamon into a bowl and stir in the sugar and raisins. Mix in the melted butter, eggs, milk and apples and beat until smooth. Turn into a greased and lined 20 cm/8 inch square cake tin.

Bake for 1-1¼ hours until the cake springs back when pressed lightly with the fingertips. Turn out to cool on a wire rack. Dust with icing sugar before serving.

72 WALNUT AND BANANA GALETTE

Preparation time:
30 minutes, plus
chilling

Cooking time:
20-25 minutes

Oven temperature:
180C/350F/gas 4

**Makes 1 x 18 cm/
7 inch galette**

Total calories:
4560

YOU WILL NEED:
175 g/6 oz butter or margarine
100 g/4 oz caster sugar
grated rind of ½ lemon
175 g/6 oz plain flour
100 g/4 oz walnuts, chopped
FOR THE FILLING AND
DECORATION
300 ml/½ pint double cream
2 tablespoons icing sugar
4 bananas
lemon juice, to sprinkle

Cream the butter or margarine, sugar and lemon rind until light and fluffy. Fold in the flour and knead into a soft dough. Place in a polythene bag and chill for 30 minutes.

Divide the dough into three. Grease and flour three baking trays and mark an 18 cm/7 inch circle on each. Place a piece of dough in each circle and press out flat to fill the circle. Sprinkle the tops with the walnuts. Bake for 20-25 minutes, then allow to cool before turning out on to a wire rack.

To decorate, whip the cream and fold in the sugar. Slice the bananas and sprinkle with lemon juice. Sandwich the layers together with cream and bananas. Pipe cream on top and decorate with banana slices. Stand 30 minutes before serving.

▬ COOK'S TIP

Unless you can be sure that your cinnamon is absolutely fresh, grind your own for this recipe. Grind 1-2 cinnamon sticks, depending upon size, in a blender, *food processor, herb mill or coffee grinder for best results.*

▬ COOK'S TIP

To make circles on the floured baking trays, use a saucepan lid of the correct size as a guide.

73 COFFEE BUTTERMILK CAKE

Preparation time:
30 minutes

Cooking time:
30 minutes

Oven temperature:
180C/350F/gas 4

Makes 1 18 cm
7 inch round cake

Total calories:
3916

YOU WILL NEED:
175 g/6 oz self-raising flour
150 g/5 oz caster sugar
5 tablespoons vegetable oil
4 tablespoons buttermilk
1 tablespoon coffee essence or
   strong black coffee
2 eggs, separated
rich buttercream (see Cook's Tip)
chocolate crisp wafers or biscuits,
   to decorate

Grease and baseline 2 18 cm/7 inch sandwich tins.

Sift the flour into a bowl, add the sugar and mix well. Add the oil, buttermilk, coffee essence or coffee and egg yolks and beat well until smooth. Whisk the egg whites until stiff and fold evenly through the mixture. Pour into the prepared tins and level the tops.

Bake in a preheated oven for 25-30 minutes, until well risen and firm to the touch. Turn out on to a wire rack and leave until cold.

Meanwhile, make the buttercream. Use about a third to sandwich the cakes together and another third to spread over the top. Put the remainder into a piping bag fitted with a star nozzle. Arrange the chocolate crisps wafers or biscuits in a wheel design on top of the cake, holding them in position with piped stars of buttercream.

◾ COOK'S TIP

For the buttercream, melt 75 g/3 oz unsalted butter in a pan. Remove from the heat and beat in 1 egg yolk, 225 g/8 oz sifted icing sugar, a few drops of *vanilla essence and enough milk to give a light spreading consistency. (You should only need a little milk.)*

74 FRUIT 'N' NUT CAKE

Preparation time:
20 minutes

Cooking time:
1¼-2 hours

Oven temperature:
150C/300F/gas 2

Makes 1 x 18 cm/
7 inch square cake

Total calories:
4475

YOU WILL NEED:
150 g/5 oz butter
6 tablespoons golden syrup
100 g/4 oz dried apricots
50 g/2 oz sultanas
225 g/8 oz raisins
100 g/4 oz currants
50 g/2 oz almonds, chopped
150 ml/¼ pint milk
225 g/8 oz plain flour
pinch of grated nutmeg
grated rind of 1 orange
2 eggs, beaten
½ teaspoon bicarbonate of soda
FOR THE TOPPING
50 g/2 oz dried apricots
50 g/2 oz whole almonds
25 g/1 oz glacé cherries
2 tablespoons honey

Put the butter, syrup, fruits, nuts and milk in a pan and melt over a low heat. Simmer gently for 5 minutes. Cool slightly. Put the flour, nutmeg and orange rind in a bowl and add the eggs. Stir the bicarbonate of soda into the cooled fruit mixture and add to the dry ingredients. Mix well and place in a greased and lined 18 cm/7 inch deep, square cake tin. Level the top.

Bake for 1¼-2 hours, then turn out to cool on a wire rack.

To make the topping, put all the ingredients in a saucepan and heat until thoroughly mixed. Spread on top of the cake.

◾ COOK'S TIP

You can test a fruit cake to see if it is cooked by inserting a fine skewer or wooden cocktail stick into the centre of the cake. If the skewer or stick comes out *clean of mixture then the cake is cooked - if not, cook longer.*

75 PASSION CAKE

Preparation time:	YOU WILL NEED:
20 minutes	*50 g/2 oz walnuts, coarsely chopped*
	2 ripe bananas, mashed
Cooking time:	*175 g/6 oz muscovado sugar*
1 hour 5 minutes	*3 eggs, beaten*
	275 g/10 oz plain flour
Oven temperature:	*1 teaspoon salt*
180C/350F/gas 4	*1 teaspoon bicarbonate of soda*
	2 teaspoons baking powder
Makes 1 x 23 cm/	*175 ml/6 fl oz corn oil*
9 inch round cake	*175 g/6 oz grated carrot*
	walnut halves, to decorate
	(optional)
Total calories:	*FOR THE ICING*
5557	*75 g/3 oz butter, softened*
	75 g/3 oz cream cheese
	175 g/6 oz icing sugar, sifted
	½ teaspoon vanilla essence

Mix the walnuts with the banana. Add the sugar and eggs and mix well. Sift the flour with the salt, bicarbonate of soda and baking powder. Add to the nut mixture with the oil and beat well. Fold in the carrot. Spoon into a greased and lined 23 cm/9 inch deep, round cake tin.

Bake for about 1 hour 5 minutes until golden and a skewer inserted into the centre comes out clean. Cool on a wire rack.

To prepare the icing, beat the butter with the cream cheese until light. Beat in the icing sugar and vanilla essence. Spread over the cake and mark with a fork to give a rough-textured finish. Decorate with walnut halves, if liked.

◼ COOK'S TIP

It is essential to use ripe bananas for this recipe. Choose bananas without a hint of green and those that have brownish streaks to their skins.

76 ORANGE TUTTI-FRUTTI CAKE

Preparation time:	YOU WILL NEED:
30 minutes	*100 g/4 oz butter*
	100 g/4 oz caster sugar
Cooking time:	*2 teaspoons finely grated orange*
1 hour	*rind*
	2 large eggs, lightly beaten
Oven temperature:	*75 g/3 oz self-raising flour*
180C/350F/gas 4	*50 g/2 oz fresh white breadcrumbs*
	50 g/2 oz prunes, stoned and
Makes 1 x 18 cm/	*finely chopped*
7 inch cake	*50 g/2 oz glacé cherries, finely*
	chopped
Total calories:	*50 g/2 oz apricots, finely chopped*
5526	*25 g/1 oz chopped mixed peel*
	1 quantity Orange Butter Icing
	(see Introduction)

Grease and base line an 18 cm/7 inch cake tin. Cream the butter, sugar and orange rind until light and fluffy. Gradually beat in the eggs, adding a tablespoon of the flour with the last amount. Sift in the flour and fold into the creamed mixture. Fold in the breadcrumbs, then the chopped fruit.

Turn the mixture into the prepared tin and level the top. Bake for 1 hour or until golden brown. Leave in the tin for 5 minutes, then turn out on to a wire rack to cool.

Spread the butter icing over the top and sides of the cake. Peel the half orange, removing all the white pith. Slice across in rings and cut each ring in half. Use to decorate the cake.

◼ COOK'S TIP

Cut off one end of an orange to make a flat base. Then remove the peel and pith together, cutting downwards with a sharp, serrated knife.

77 CHOCOLATE SWISS ROLL

Preparation time:
20 minutes

Cooking time:
7-10 minutes

Oven temperature:
200C/400F/gas 6

Makes one Swiss Roll

Total calories:
1433

YOU WILL NEED:
2 large eggs
50 g/2 oz caster sugar
50 g/2 oz self-raising flour, less
  1 tablespoon
1 tablespoon cocoa powder
extra caster sugar, to dredge
FOR THE FILLING
50 g/2 oz butter
75 g/3 oz icing sugar, sieved
few drops peppermint essence

Grease a 28 x 18 cm/11 x 7 inch Swiss roll tin and line the base and sides with greased greaseproof paper. Whisk the eggs and sugar together until they are light and creamy and the whisk leaves a trail when it is lifted out. Sift in the flour and cocoa, then fold into the mixture. Turn into the prepared tin and level off the top.

Bake for 7-10 minutes until the cake springs back when pressed lightly. Turn out on to a piece of greaseproof paper dredged with caster sugar. Trim off the edges and quickly roll up the Swiss roll, keeping it wrapped in the greaseproof paper. Leave to cool.

Cream the butter and icing sugar together, then beat in the peppermint essence. Unroll the cake, removing the greaseproof paper, spread with the peppermint butter cream, then re-roll. Dredge the outside of the roll with caster sugar before serving.

■ COOK'S TIP

It is easier to spread butter cream smoothly if you use a small palette knife dipped in hot water.

78 CHOCOLATE BATTENBURG

Preparation time:
about 40 minutes

Cooking time:
about 30 minutes

Oven temperature:
180C/350F/gas 4

**Makes 1 x 20 cm/
8 inch square cake**

Total calories:
4456 per portion

YOU WILL NEED:
100 g/4 oz butter or hard margarine
100 g/4 oz caster sugar
2 eggs
100 g/4 oz self-raising flour, sifted
1 teaspoon coffee essence
2 teaspoons cocoa powder
1 quantity Chocolate Butter
  Cream (see Introduction)
175-225 g/6-8 oz white marzipan
a few chocolate coffee matchsticks

Prepare a cake tin (see Cook's Tip). Use the fat, sugar, eggs and flour to make a Victoria sandwich (recipe 93). Divide the mixture in half and add the coffee essence to one portion and the cocoa to the other. Place the mixtures in the tin. Bake for about 30 minutes, until well-risen and firm. Turn on to a wire rack to go cold. Remove the paper and stand one piece of cake on the other. Trim, cut in half lengthwise and reverse so the two flavours are opposite. Spread butter cream over the pieces and stick them together. Spread butter cream around the sides.

Roll out the marzipan to a rectangle big enough to enclose the cake. Stand the cake on top and wrap the marzipan around it, join underneath. Trim the ends. Pinch a 'finger and thumb' design along the edges. Mark a criss-cross along the top. Pipe butter cream along the top and add chocolate matchsticks.

■ COOK'S TIP

Grease and line a 20 cm/8 inch square tin for this cake, making a pleat in the lining down the centre which stands up about 4 cm/1 ½ inches. This divides *the tin so that both flavours can be baked at the same time.*

79 MANDARIN CLOUD

Preparation time: 25 minutes	YOU WILL NEED: *150 g/5 oz plain flour* *25 g/1 oz cornflour*
Cooking time: 25-30 minutes	*2 teaspoons baking powder* *150 g/5 oz icing sugar* *5 tablespoons oil*
Oven temperature: 190C/375F/gas 5	*6 tablespoons water* *3 eggs, separated* *finely grated rind and juice of*
Makes 1 x 20 cm/ **8 inch layer cake**	*1 orange* *FILLING AND DECORATION* *3 tablespoons ground almonds*
Total calories: 4242	*2 tablespoons icing sugar, sifted* *1 tablespoon orange juice* *450 ml/¾ pint double cream,* *whipped* *1 x 212 g/7½ oz can mandarin* *oranges, drained*

Sift the flour with the cornflour, baking powder and icing sugar. Beat the oil, water and egg yolks together lightly and beat into the dry ingredients. Stir in the orange rind and juice. Whisk the egg whites until stiff and fold into the cake mixture.

Pour into 2 greased and lined 20 cm/8 inch sandwich tins. Bake for 25-30 minutes until well-risen and just firm. Leave in the tins for 10 minutes, then cool on a wire rack.

Whisk the almonds, sugar and juice into two-thirds of the whipped cream. Sandwich the cakes together with half and use the rest to cover the cake. Pipe the remaining whipped cream around the top edge of the cake and decorate with mandarins.

COOK'S TIP

You may use fresh mandarins or tangerines for this cake. You will need the segmented flesh of about 4-5 fruit, depending upon size.

80 CHOCOLATE ALMOND TORTE

Preparation time: 20 minutes	YOU WILL NEED: *100 g/4 oz plain flour* *¼ teaspoon baking powder*
Cooking time: 35 minutes	*¼ teaspoon bicarbonate of soda* *40 g/1½ oz cocoa powder* *75 g/3 oz butter*
Oven temperature: 190C/375F/gas 5	*150 g/5 oz soft brown sugar* *2 eggs* *3 tablespoons soured cream*
Makes 1 x 20 cm/ **8 in round cake**	*¼ teaspoon almond essence* *300 ml/½ pint double cream* *100 g/4 oz chocolate caraque*
Total calories: 3849	*(see recipe 160)*

Sift together the flour, baking powder, bicarbonate of soda and cocoa. Cream the butter and sugar together until light, then gradually beat in the eggs, soured cream and almond essence. Fold in the dry ingredients.

Turn into a greased and lined 20 cm/8 inch round cake tin and level the surface. Bake for about 35 minutes, until firm. Leave the cake in the tin to cool, then turn out.

Whip the cream, then swirl over the cake. Top with the chocolate caraque.

COOK'S TIP

During folding, take care not to disturb all the air that has been introduced during the creaming process - a simple stir or, worse still, beating, would break the bubbles and let out the air. Fold mixtures with a metal spoon that will cut neatly through the mixture, disturbing the air bubbles as little as possible.

81 DEVIL'S FOOD CAKE

Preparation time:
20-30 minutes

Cooking time:
1¼-2 hours

Oven temperature:
150C/300F/gas 2

**Makes 1 x 20 cm/
8 inch round cake**

Total calories:
4565

YOU WILL NEED:
175 g/6 oz butter or margarine
175 g/6 oz soft brown sugar
2 eggs
175 g/6 oz golden syrup
50 g/2 oz ground almonds
175 g/6 oz plain flour
50 g/2 oz cocoa powder
175 ml/6 fl oz milk
¼ teaspoon bicarbonate of soda
1 quantity American frosting
 (see Introduction)
chocolate curls (see recipe 162),
 to decorate

Cream the butter and sugar together until light and fluffy. Add the remaining cake ingredients and beat well with a wooden spoon. Pour into a greased and lined 20 cm/8 inch deep round cake tin.

Bake for 1¼-2 hours, the turn out to cool on a wire rack.

To decorate the cake, spread the frosting over it, making deep swirls with a palette knife. Decorate with chocolate curls.

82 CHOCOLATE BUTTERMILK CAKE

Preparation time:
30 minutes

Cooking time:
about 30 minutes

Oven temperature:
180C/350F/gas 4

**Makes 1 x 18 cm/
7 inch layer cake**

Total calories:
3538

YOU WILL NEED:
150 g/5 oz self-raising flour
25 g/1 oz cocoa or carob powder
150 g/5 oz caster sugar
5 tablespoons vegetable oil
5 tablespoons buttermilk
2 eggs, separated
crème au beurre (see Cook's Tip)
chocolate crisp wafers, to decorate

Sift the flour and cocoa or carob powder into a bowl, add the sugar and mix well. Add the oil, buttermilk and egg yolks and beat well until smooth, about 2 minutes with an electric mixer or 3 minutes by hand. Whisk the egg whites until stiff and fold evenly through the mixture. Pour into 2 greased and base-lined 18 cm/7 inch sandwich tins and level the tops. Bake for 25-30 minutes or until well-risen and firm to the touch. Turn out on to a wire rack and leave until cold.

Make the crème au beurre. Use a third of the mixture to sandwich the cakes, a third to spread over the top; put the remainder into a piping bag fitted with a star nozzle. Attach the chocolate wafers to the cake with stars of butter cream.

■ COOK'S TIP

If you do not intend to eat this cake immediately, it will keep well un-iced in an airtight container. Once the cake is iced, it should be eaten as soon as possible.

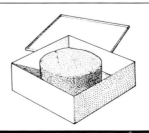

■ COOK'S TIP

For crème au beurre, melt 75 g/3 oz un salted butter, take off heat and gradually beat in 1 egg yolk, 225 g/8 oz sifted icing sugar, a few drops vanilla essence and *sufficient milk to give a light spreading consistency.*

83   CHOCOLATE LAYER CAKE

Preparation time:
30 minutes

Cooking time:
30-40 minutes

Oven temperature:
160C/325F/gas 3

**Makes 1 x 18 cm/
7 inch cake**

Total calories:
4396

YOU WILL NEED:
1 tablespoon cocoa powder
1 tablespoon hot water
175 g/6 oz butter or margarine,
* softened*
175 g/6 oz caster sugar
3 eggs
175 g/6 oz self-raising flour
1½ teaspoons baking powder
FOR THE ICING AND
DECORATION
225 g/8 oz Chocolate Butter Icing
* (see Introduction)*
brandy (optional)
chocolate vermicelli
chocolate shapes

Mix the cocoa with the hot water and allow to cool. Place all the ingredients for the cake in a bowl and beat with a wooden spoon until well mixed. Divide the mixture between 2 greased and base-lined 18 cm/7 inch sandwich tins. Bake for 30-40 minutes, then turn out to cool on a wire rack.

To decorate the cake, mix the chocolate icing with a little brandy if liked. Spread two-thirds over the top and sides of the cake, using a decorative scraper if liked to give a ridged effect. Roll the sides of the cake in chocolate vermicelli to coat. Place the remainder in a piping bag fitted with a star nozzle and pipe swirls of icing around the edge of the cake. Decorate with chocolate shapes as shown.

▧ COOK'S TIP

To achieve the decoration shown on top of the cake, hold the scraper at an angle of about 45° to the cake and press just hard enough to indent the surface.

84   BOOTLEGGER'S CAKE

Preparation time:
15 minutes

Cooking time:
1½ hours

Oven temperature:
160C/325F/gas 3

**Makes 1 x 23 cm/
9 inch round cake**

Total calories:
6540

YOU WILL NEED:
250 ml/8 fl oz milk
1 tablespoon lemon juice
200 ml/7 fl oz golden syrup
100 g/4 oz caster sugar
2 eggs, lightly beaten
375 g/13 oz plain flour
2 teaspoons bicarbonate of soda
1 teaspoon baking powder
1 teaspoon ground cinnamon
1 teaspoon ground ginger
250 g/9 oz shredded suet
200 g/7 oz walnuts, chopped
275 g/ 10 oz raisins, chopped
120 ml/4 fl oz bourbon, whisky or
* rum*
moonshine glaze (see Cook's Tip)

Grease and flour a 23 cm/9 inch deep, round cake tin. Mix the milk and lemon juice and let stand 5 minutes. Stir together the golden syrup, sugar and eggs.

Sift the flour, bicarbonate of soda, baking powder and spices together. Tip about a third of the mixture into a bowl and stir in the suet, nuts and raisins. Sift the remaining flour mixture into the golden syrup mixture, alternating with the milk. Stir in the alcohol, then the suet, nuts and raisins. Pour into the prepared tin and bake in a preheated oven until the top of the cake is firm and cracked open (about 1½ hours.) Let the cake cool for 10 minutes in the tin on a wire rack, then turn out and spoon over the glaze. Cool before serving.

▧ COOK'S TIP

For the moonshine glaze, mix together until smooth 100 g/4 oz sifted icing sugar, 25 g/1 oz softened butter, 2 teaspoons of the alcohol chosen for the cake and 1 teaspoon vanilla essence. The mixture should be of a consistency to drip in glossy runnels down the side of the cake.

85   HONEY WALNUT ROULADE

Preparation time:	YOU WILL NEED:
20-25 minutes	*3 large eggs, separated*
	2 teaspoons water
Cooking time:	*75 g/3 oz caster sugar*
12-14 minutes	*2 tablespoons clear honey*
	100 g/4 oz self-raising flour
Oven temperature:	*75 g/3 oz ground walnuts*
200C/400F/gas 6	*caster sugar, to sprinkle*
	whipped cream and walnut
Serves 4-6	* halves, to decorate*
	FOR THE FILLING
Calories:	*150 ml/¼ pint double cream*
558-372 per portion	*25 g/1 oz walnut pieces*
	1 tablespoon clear honey

Whisk the egg whites with the water until very stiff. Gradually add the sugar, a spoonful at a time, and whisk until thick and glossy. Whisk in the egg yolks and honey, then fold in the flour and ground walnuts with a metal spoon. Turn into a greased, lined and floured 28 x 24/11 x 9 ½ inch Swiss roll tin and level the surface.

Bake for 12-14 minutes, then turn out quickly on to a sheet of greaseproof paper sprinkled with caster sugar. Trim the edges with a sharp knife and then roll up like a Swiss roll, enclosing the paper. Leave until cold.

To make the filling, whip the cream, then fold in the walnut pieces and honey. Unroll the roulade and remove the paper. Spread with the filling and re-roll. Decorate with whipped cream and walnut halves.

■ COOK'S TIP

Ground walnuts are rarely sold but you can easily make your own in a food processor or blender. Simply grind the walnuts using the metal blade for a few seconds until just powdery.

86   NEVER-FAIL SPONGE CAKE

Preparation time:	YOU WILL NEED:
20 minutes	*225 g/8 oz caster sugar*
	3 large eggs
Cooking time:	*50 g/2 oz butter*
20-25 minutes	*3 tablespoons water*
	½ teaspoon vanilla essence
Oven temperature:	*150 g/5 oz plain flour*
190C/375F/gas 5	*3 tablespoons jam*
	sifted icing sugar
Makes 1 x 18 cm/	
7 inch round	
sandwich cake	
Total calories:	
2237	

Grease and base-line 2 18 cm/7 inch sandwich tins. Whisk the sugar and eggs together with an electric beater for 10 minutes. Put the butter and water into a small pan and heat gently until the butter has melted. Pour into the whisked mixture with the vanilla essence and whisk for just half a minute. Sift the flour and fold into the mixture.

Turn into the prepared tins and give each tin a sharp tap to settle the mixture. Bake for 20-25 minutes or until well-risen and the cakes spring back when pressed lightly. Leave in the tins for 2-3 minutes, then turn out on to a wire rack to cool. When cold sandwich together with the jam and dust the top with icing sugar.

■ COOK'S TIP

The quickest way to grease cake tins is to use a pastry brush dipped in light vegetable oil. The mixture is less likely to stick than if fat is used.

87 OLD-FASHIONED MADEIRA CAKE

Preparation time:
15-20 minutes

Cooking time:
1¼-1½ hours

Oven temperature:
160C/325F/gas 3

**Makes 1 x 18 cm/
7 inch round cake**

Total calories:
3061

YOU WILL NEED:
175 g/6 oz butter
175 g/6 oz caster sugar
grated rind of 1 lemon
3 eggs
225 g/8 oz plain flour
1½ teaspoons baking powder
2 tablespoons warm water
piece of candied peel

Cream the butter, sugar and lemon rind together until light and fluffy. Beat in the eggs, one at a time, adding a little of the flour with each egg after the first. Fold in the remaining flour and baking powder using a metal spoon. Fold in the water gently to give a soft, dropping consistency. Place in a greased and base-lined 18 cm/7 inch deep cake tin. Place the candied peel in the centre of the cake.

Bake for 1¼-1½ hours. Allow to cool slightly in the tin before turning out to cool on a wire rack.

88 COUNTRY FRUIT CAKE

Preparation time:
20 minutes

Cooking time:
1 hour

Oven temperature:
190C/375F/gas 5

**Makes 1 x 18 cm/
7 inch cake**

Total calories:
2824

YOU WILL NEED:
225 g/8 oz self-raising flour
pinch of salt
½ teaspoon ground mixed spice
75 g/3 oz margarine
100 g/4 oz soft brown sugar
100 g/4 oz raisins
100 g/4 oz sultanas
50 g/2 oz chopped mixed peel
50 g/2 oz glacé cherries, chopped
1 large egg, lightly beaten
about 150 ml/¼ pint milk

Grease an 18 cm/7 inch cake tin thoroughly and line the base with greased greaseproof paper. Sift together the flour, salt and spice. Rub in the margarine. Add the sugar, raisins, sultanas, peel and cherries. Add the egg and sufficient milk so that the mixture will drop from a spoon when shaken.

Turn into the prepared tin. Bake for 1 hour or until the cake is golden and a skewer inserted into the centre comes out clean. Leave in the tin for 5 minutes, turn out on to a wire rack and cool.

■ COOK'S TIP

Cakes are called rich, plain or sponge depending upon how much fat, flour, sugar and eggs they have. This is a rich cake, made by the creaming method; it has almost equal quantities of fat and flour, and is rich in eggs and sugar.

■ COOK'S TIP

If you often use the same tin for baking cakes, it is a good idea to cut out several layers of greaseproof paper in the required size and store them.

89   CORNISH SAFFRON CAKE

Preparation time:
20 minutes, plus
rising

Cooking time:
1 hour

Oven temperature:
200C/400F/gas 6
180C/350F/gas 4

**Makes 1 x 20 cm/
8 inch round cake**

Total calories:
3414

YOU WILL NEED:
1 teaspoon sugar
scant 300 ml/½ pint warm milk
2 teaspoons dried yeast
1 small sachet powdered saffron
*   or few strands saffron*
150 ml/¼ pint boiling water
450 g/1 lb plain flour
1 teaspoon salt
100 g/4 oz margarine
25g/1 oz caster sugar
175 g/6 oz currants
100 g/4 oz chopped mixed peel

Grease a 20 cm/8 inch round cake tin. Dissolve the sugar in the warm milk, sprinkle over the dried yeast and leave for about 10 minutes or until frothy. Pour the boiling water over the saffron and leave to cool. Strain if using saffron strands.

Sift the flour and salt and rub in the margarine. Add the sugar, currants and peel. Add the saffron liquid and the yeast liquid and mix to a soft dough. Turn into the prepared cake tin and cover with a damp cloth. Leave to rise until the dough comes to the top of the tin - 1 hour in a warm place or 2 hours at average room temperature.

Remove the cloth and bake at the higher temperature for 30 minutes, reduce the temperature and bake for 30 minutes. Leave in the tin 2-3 minutes, turn out and cool on a wire rack.

▮ COOK'S TIP

*Traditionally the saffron
cake mixture was baked in
a loaf tin and served cut in
slices spread with butter.*

90   BOILED FRUIT CAKE

Preparation time:
15-20 minutes

Cooking time:
1½ hours

Oven temperature:
180C/350F/gas 4

**Makes 1 x 15 cm/
6 inch round cake**

Total calories:
2170

YOU WILL NEED:
175g/6 oz mixed dried fruit
75 g/3 oz margarine
75 g/3 oz soft brown sugar
1 teaspoon ground mixed spiced
200 ml/7 fl oz water
225 g/8 oz plain flour
1 teaspoon bicarbonate of soda
½ teaspoon salt

Grease a 15 cm/6 inch cake tin and line the base and sides with greased greaseproof paper. Put the diced fruit, margarine, sugar, spice and water in a pan. Bring to the boil and boil for 3 minutes. Allow to cool. Sift the flour, bicarbonate of soda and salt together and pour in the boiled mixture. Beat well and turn into the prepared tin.

Bake for 1½ hours or until a skewer inserted into the centre comes out clean. Leave in the tin for 5 minutes, then turn out on to a wire rack to cool.

▮ COOK'S TIP

*If brown sugar becomes
caked, cover the open
packet with a damp piece of
absorbent kitchen paper
and put in a polythene bag.
Leave for a few hours and*
*the sugar will be moist
again.*

91 DUNDEE CAKE

Preparation time:	YOU WILL NEED:
20 minutes	175 g/6 oz butter
	175 g/6 oz soft brown sugar
Cooking time:	3 large eggs, lightly beaten
2½ hours	175 g/6 oz plain flour
	25 g/1 oz ground almonds
Oven temperature:	1 teaspoon baking powder
180C/350F/gas 4;	225 g/8 oz sultanas
150C/300F/gas 2	225 g/8 oz currants
	75 g/3 oz chopped mix peel
	75 g/3 oz glacé cherries, halved
Makes 1 x 18 cm/	1 teaspoon finely grated lemon rind
7 inch round cake	1½ tablespoons lemon juice
	about 20 split blanched almonds
Total calories:	
3837	

Grease an 18 cm/7 inch round cake tin and line the base and sides with greased greaseproof paper. Cream the butter and sugar until light and fluffy. Gradually beat in the eggs, adding a tablespoon of the flour with the last amount. Fold in the almonds. Sift in the remaining flour and baking powder and fold into the creamed mixture with the dried fruit, peel, cherries, lemon rind and juice.

Turn into the prepared tin and level off. Arrange the almonds on the top of the cake and brush with a little egg white. Bake at the higher temperature for 1 hour, then reduce the temperature and bake for a further 1½ hours or until a skewer inserted in the centre comes out clean. Leave the cake in the tin for 10 minutes, then carefully turn out on to a wire rack to cool.

▨ COOK'S TIP

You can get enough egg white to brush the almonds on top of the cake by brushing the inside of the egg shells.

92 FROSTED COFFEE CAKE

Preparation time:	YOU WILL NEED:
20 minutes	175 g/6 oz butter or margarine
	175 g/6 oz caster sugar
Cooking time:	3 eggs, beaten
30 minutes	175 g/6 oz self-raising flour
	2 tablespoons strong black coffee
Oven temperature:	1 quantity Coffee icing
180C/350F/gas 4	(see Cook's Tip)
Makes 1 x 20 cm/	
8 inch round	
sandwich cake	
Total calories:	
4058	

Mix the butter and sugar in a bowl with a wooden spoon, then beat until light and fluffy. Add the beaten eggs a little at a time, beating well between each addition. Add the flour and fold in lightly with a metal tablespoon, cutting through the mixture and turning it over until the flour is evenly mixed. Fold in the coffee lightly.

Divide the mixture between 2 greased and base-lined 20 cm/8 inch round sandwich tins. Level the tops with the back of a metal spoon. Bake for 30 minutes until the cakes are golden brown and spring back when pressed lightly. Turn out the cakes, remove the lining paper and cool on a wire rack.

Place one cake on a serving plate, spread with half the icing and cover with the other cake. Spread the top with the remaining icing, swirling with a round-ended knife.

▨ COOK'S TIP

Put 225 g/8 oz sifted icing sugar, 50 g/2 oz butter and 2 tablespoons strong black coffee in a bowl over a pan of hot water. Heat gently, stirring until smooth and *glossy. Leave the icing until cold, then beat until thick enough to spread.*

93   VICTORIA SANDWICH

Preparation time:
15-20 minutes

Cooking time:
20-25 minutes

Oven temperature:
180C/350F/gas 4

**Makes 1 x 18 cm/
7 inch round
sandwich cake**

Total calories:
1605

YOU WILL NEED:
100 g/4 oz butter or margarine
100 g/4 oz caster sugar
2 eggs
100 g/4 oz self-raising flour, sifted
1 tablespoon hot water
raspberry jam
sifted icing sugar

Cream the butter or margarine and sugar together until light and fluffy. Beat in the eggs, one at a time, adding a tablespoon of the flour with the second egg. Fold in the remaining flour, then the hot water.

Turn the mixture into 2 greased and base-lined 18 cm/7 inch sandwich tins. Bake for 20-25 minutes or until the cakes spring back when pressed lightly. Turn out on to a wire rack to cool.

Fill with raspberry jam and dust with icing sugar.

94   CHOCOLATE AND ALMOND SANDWICH

Preparation time:
20-25 minutes

Cooking time:
20-25 minutes

Oven temperature:
180C/350F/gas 4

**Makes 1 x 18 cm/
7 inch round
sandwich cake**

Total calories:
3552

YOU WILL NEED:
100 g/4 oz butter or margarine
100 g/4 oz caster sugar
2 eggs
100 g/4 oz self-raising flour
¼ teaspoon almond essence
1 tablespoon hot water
FOR THE FILLING AND TOPPING
*1 quantity Chocolate Butter icing
  (see Introduction)*
50 g/2 oz flaked almonds, toasted

Use the ingredients to make a Victoria sponge (see recipe 93), adding the almond essence with the hot water. Turn the mixture into 2 greased and base-lined 18 cm/7 inch sandwich tins. Bake for 20-25 minutes or until the cakes spring back when pressed lightly. Turn out on to a wire rack to cool.

Spread one cake with a third of the chocolate butter icing and cover with 2 tablespoons chopped toasted almonds. Press the other cake on top and ruffle on the remaining icing. Decorate the edge with a ring of flaked almonds and arrange the remainder in the centre.

■ COOK'S TIP

To make a coffee sandwich simply add 1 tablespoon coffee powder with the flour. To make an orange or lemon sandwich cake, add the grated rind of 1 orange or lemon with the butter and sugar.

■ COOK'S TIP

Caster sugar is preferable to granulated sugar for most cakes as it creams smoothly and melts easily during baking.

95 ALMOND LAYER CAKE

Preparation time:
25-30 minutes

Cooking time:
20 minutes

Oven temperature:
190C/375F/gas 5

Makes 1 x 30 x 12.5 cm/12 x 5 inch layer cake

Total calories:
3419

YOU WILL NEED:
4 large eggs
100 g/4 oz caster sugar
75 g/3 oz self-raising flour
50 g/2 oz ground almonds
few drops almond essence
50 g/2 oz toasted flaked almonds
FOR THE ICING
3 egg whites
500 g/18 oz caster sugar
pinch of salt
6 tablespoons cold water
pinch of cream of tartar

Whisk the eggs and sugar until the mixture is thick and creamy and the whisk leaves a trail when it is lifted out. Sift in the flour and fold into the mixture with the ground almonds and the almond essence. Turn the mixture into a greased and lined roasting tin about 38 x 30 cm/15 x 12 inch and level off. Bake for 20 minutes or until the cake springs back when pressed lightly. Turn out on to a sheet of greaseproof paper and leave until cold. Then cut it across into three rectangles.

Put the icing ingredients into a bowl over a pan of hot water. Beat (preferably with an electric hand beater) until the mixture thickens. Spread some of the icing on two of the rectangles of cake, sprinkle with some of the almonds and sandwich together. Spread the remaining icing over the top and sides of the cake and sprinkle with the remaining almonds.

COOK'S TIP

You should leave this cake to set for at least 1 hour in a cool place before cutting it with a sharp serrated knife.

96 STICKY GINGERBREAD

Preparation time:
15 minutes

Cooking time:
45 minutes

Oven temperature:
180C/350F/gas 4

Makes about 15

Calories:
247 per slice

YOU WILL NEED:
275 g/10 oz plain flour
2 teaspoons ground ginger
1 teaspoon bicarbonate of soda
100 g/4 oz margarine
100 g/4 oz soft light brown sugar
225 g/8 oz golden syrup
100 g/4 oz black treacle
2 eggs, beaten
150 ml/¼ pint hot water

Grease and line a 30 x 23 cm/12 x 9 inch roasting tin. Sift the flour, ginger and bicarbonate of soda into a large mixing bowl. Put the margarine, sugar, syrup and treacle in a saucepan. Heat gently until the margarine has melted and the sugar has dissolved.

Make a well in the centre of the dry ingredients. Pour the mixture from the saucepan into the flour and beat well to mix. Add the beaten eggs and hot water and mix to a smooth batter. Pour the mixture into the prepared tin. Bake for 45 minutes until the cake springs back when pressed lightly. Turn out of the tin, remove the lining paper and cool on a wire rack.

COOK'S TIP

Wrapped in greaseproof paper and then in foil, this gingerbread will keep for up to two weeks. In any case, it should be kept for two days before being cut.

97 MONSIEUR AUDAT'S GOOSEBERRY CAKE

Preparation time:
15 minutes

Cooking time:
about 45 minutes

Oven temperature:
180C/350F/gas 4

Makes 1 x 18-19 cm/7-7½ inch deep round cake

Total calories:
1939

YOU WILL NEED:
100 g/4 oz butter or hard
  margarine
165 g/5½ oz self-raising flour
1 teaspoon baking powder
2 eggs, beaten
100 g/4 oz caster sugar
1½ tablespoons white wine
1½ teaspoons orange-flower or
  rose water
½ teaspoon grated or ground
  nutmeg
100 g/4 oz gooseberries, topped
  and tailed
caster sugar, to dredge

Grease and line an 18-19 cm/7-7½ inch round spring release cake tin. Melt the butter or margarine in a saucepan and then cool until only just warm. Sift in the flour and baking powder and mix into the butter or margarine with the eggs, sugar, wine, flavouring and nutmeg; beat well.

Pour half the mixture into the prepared tin, cover with the gooseberries and then add the remaining mixture, making sure the gooseberries are covered. Bake for about 45 minutes or until golden brown and a skewer inserted in the centre comes out clean. Cool in the tin for a few minutes, then remove carefully on to a wire rack. Dredge with caster sugar and leave until cold.

■ COOK'S TIP

Orange-flower or rose water is available from well-stocked delicatessens and traditional grocers. Some chemists also sell it.

98 AMERICAN CARROT CAKE

Preparation time:
20-25 minutes

Cooking time:
1½ hours

Oven temperature:
180C/350F/gas 4

Makes 1 x 20 cm/ 8 inch cake

Total calories:
5279

YOU WILL NEED:
225 g/8 oz butter
225 g/8 oz caster sugar
4 eggs, beaten
225 g/8 oz self-raising flour
grated rind of 1 lemon
2 tablespoons lemon juice
1 tablespoon Kirsch
225 g/8 oz carrots, grated
100 g/4 oz blanched almonds,
  finely chopped
marzipan and angelica, to
  decorate
FOR THE LEMON ICING
225 g/8 oz icing sugar, sifted
5 teaspoons lemon juice

Cream the butter and sugar together until light and fluffy. Beat in the eggs with a little of the flour, then fold in the remaining flour with the lemon rind, lemon juice and Kirsch. Add the carrots and almonds, mix well. Spoon into a greased and lined 20 cm/8 inch deep, round cake tin.

Bake for 1½ hours until well-risen, golden and firm to the touch. Turn out to cool on a wire rack.

To make the icing, mix the icing sugar with the lemon juice until smooth and glossy. Pour over the top of the cooled cake, allowing it to run down the sides. Decorate with marzipan (coloured orange, if liked) shaped into carrots with green angelica tops.

■ COOK'S TIP

To colour marzipan, just add a few drops of the chosen food colouring to the marzipan ball and knead until the colour is uniformly mixed into the *paste. Leave the shapes to dry slightly before adding to the cake so that the colours do not run into the icing.*

99 APRICOT BUTTERSCOTCH CAKE

Preparation time:	YOU WILL NEED:
30 minutes	175 g/6 oz butter
	75 g/3 oz light soft brown sugar
Cooking time:	75 g/3 oz dark soft brown sugar
20-25 minutes	3 eggs
	175 g/6 oz self-raising flour, sifted
Oven temperature:	1 tablespoon black treacle
190C/375F/gas 5	1 tablespoon lemon juice
	FOR THE FILLING
Makes 1 x 20 cm/	1 x 425 g/15 oz can apricot halves,
8 inch square cake	drained
	150 ml/¼ pint double or
Total calories:	whipping cream
3658	3 tablespoons milk

Grease and line two 20 cm/8 inch square sandwich tins. Use the butter, sugar, eggs, and flour to make a Victoria sandwich (see recipe 93), then beat in the black treacle and lemon juice. Divide the mixture between the tins, levelling the tops and making sure there is sufficient mixture in the corners. Bake for 20 minutes, until well-risen, golden and just firm to the touch. Turn out to cool on a wire rack. Peel off the lining paper.

For the filling, chop half the apricots and cut the rest into quarters. Whip the cream and milk together until stiff. Put almost half into a piping bag with a 1 cm/½ inch plain nozzle. Fold the remainder into the chopped apricots. Sandwich the cakes together with the apricot cream. Pipe a lattice of cream over the top and fill alternate squares with the apricot quarters.

▨ COOK'S TIP

The cakes can be wrapped in foil and frozen for up to 3 months. When thawed, fill with the apricot cream and decorate.

100 APPLE CAKE

Preparation time:	YOU WILL NEED:
15 minutes	225 g/8 oz self-raising flour
	1 teaspoon salt
Cooking time:	100 g/4 oz butter
30-40 minutes	450 g/1 lb cooking or dessert
	apples, peeled, cored and
Oven temperature:	chopped
200C/400F/gas 6	100 g/4 oz caster sugar
	2 eggs, beaten
Makes 1 x 20-23	25 g/1 oz soft brown sugar
cm/8-9 inch cake	
Total calories:	
2504	

Sift the flour and salt into a mixing bowl. Cut the butter into the flour and rub in to a breadcrumb consistency. Mix in the apples, caster sugar and eggs.

Turn into a greased 20-23 cm/8-9 inch cake tin. Level off the top and sprinkle with the brown sugar. Bake for 30-40 minutes. Allow to shrink slightly before turning out.

▨ COOK'S TIP

This cake can be served while still hot with clotted cream. Alternatively, cool on a wire rack and serve with butter.

101 TEISEN LAP

Preparation time:
15 minutes

Cooking time:
about 1 hour

Oven temperature:
180C/350F/gas 4;
then
140C/275F/gas 1

Makes 1 x 20-23 cm/8-9 inch plate cake

Total calories:
2892

YOU WILL NEED:
225 g/8 oz plain flour
2 teaspoons baking powder
½ teaspoon grated nutmeg
50 g/2 oz butter
50 g/2 oz lard
100 g/4 oz soft brown sugar
100 g/4 oz mixed dried fruit
2 eggs, beaten
about 150 ml/¼ pint buttermilk
    or single cream

Sift the flour, baking powder and nutmeg into a mixing bowl. Cut the fats into the flour and rub in to a breadcrumb consistency. Mix in the sugar and dried fruit. Stir in the eggs and sufficient buttermilk or cream to make a soft dough.

Turn into a shallow greased 20-23 cm/8-9 inch tin. Bake at the higher temperature for 20-30 minutes until risen and set. Then reduce the temperature and bake for a further 40 minutes or until a skewer inserted in the cake comes out clean.

■ COOK'S TIP

In some parts of Wales a slightly firmer dough is rolled out to 2.5 cm/1 inch thickness, cut into 6 cm/2½ inch rounds and then cooked on a warmed greased bakestone or griddle for about 15 minutes on each side.

102 PORTER CAKE

Preparation time:
20 minutes

Cooking time:
about 3 hours

Oven temperature:
140C/275F/gas 1;
120C/250F/gas ½

Makes one 20 cm/ 8 inch cake

Total calories:
5363

YOU WILL NEED:
350 g/12 oz plain flour
¼ teaspoon mixed spice
175 g/6 oz butter or margarine
275 g/10 oz soft brown sugar
450 g/1 lb mixed dried fruit
50 g/2 oz glacé cherries
50 g/2 oz walnuts, chopped or
    2 oz blanched almonds, shredded
grated rind of 1 lemon
½ teaspoon bicarbonate of soda
150 ml/¼ pint warm stout
3 eggs, beaten

Grease and line a 20 cm/8 inch round cake tin and tie a band of brown paper round the outside of the tin and 5 cm/2 inches above it to protect the top of the cake during baking.

Sift the flour and mixed spiced into a mixing bowl. Cut the fat into the flour and rub in to a breadcrumb consistency. Stir in the sugar, fruit, nuts and grated lemon rind and mix well. Dissolve the bicarbonate of soda in the warm stout and add to the beaten eggs. Stir this into the dry ingredients and mix well.

Pour into the prepared tin and bake in the centre of the oven at the higher temperature for 2 hours or until set. Reduce the temperature and bake for a further hour or until a skewer inserted comes out clean. Leave to cool in the tin.

■ COOK'S TIP

The cake is named after the type of stout that was traditionally used in Ireland. It is best if allowed to mature for a few days in an airtight tin.

103 SCOTS SEED CAKE

Preparation time:	YOU WILL NEED:
20 minutes	*100 g/4 oz butter or margarine*
	100 g/4 oz caster sugar
Cooking time:	*2 large eggs, separated*
1½ hours	*1 tablespoon whisky or brandy*
	100 g/4 oz plain flour
Oven temperature:	*¼ teaspoon baking powder*
160C/325F/gas 3	*¼ teaspoon grated nutmeg*
	50 g/2 oz blanched almonds,
Makes 1 x 15 cm/	*shredded*
6 inch cake	*50 g/2 oz candied orange peel,*
	chopped
Total calories:	*25 g/1 oz candied citron peel,*
2317	*chopped*
	caraway seeds, to sprinkle
	granulated sugar, to sprinkle

Line the sides and base of a round 15 cm/6 inch cake tin with greased greaseproof paper. Cream the fat and sugar until light and fluffy. Gradually beat in the egg yolks. Whisk the egg whites until stiff but not brittle, and fold in alternately with the flour, sifted with the baking powder and nutmeg. Fold in the almonds, candied peel and whisky or brandy. Turn into the prepared tin. Sprinkle with caraway seeds and granulated sugar.

Bake in the centre of the oven for 1½ hours or until set and golden. Test with a skewer. Allow the cake to shrink slightly, then turn out on to a wire rack, remove the lining paper and leave to cool.

▪ COOK'S TIP

The top of this cake was traditionally decorated with caraway comfits, which were supposed to be beneficial for the digestion. If preferred, ¼ teaspoon *round caraway seeds can be mixed in with the flour.*

104 ORANGE CURD CAKE

Preparation time:	YOU WILL NEED:
20-25 minutes	*100 g/4 oz self-raising flour*
	1 teaspoon baking powder
Cooking time:	*100 g/4 oz caster sugar*
30 minutes	*100 g/4 oz soft margarine*
	2 eggs
Oven temperature:	*grated rind of 1 orange*
180C/350F/gas 4	*FOR THE FILLING AND*
	DECORATION
Makes 1 x 18 cm/7	*2 oranges*
inch sandwich cake	*25 g/1 oz caster sugar*
	100 g/4 oz curd cheese
Total calories:	*caster sugar, to sprinkle*
2185	

Grease and base-line two 18 cm/7 inch sandwich cake tins. Put the flour, baking powder, sugar, margarine, eggs and orange rind in a bowl. Beat with a wooden spoon until light and fluffy, about 3 minutes (or 1 minute with a mixer). Divide the mixture between the prepared cake tins and smooth the tops.

Bake for 30 minutes, until the cakes are golden brown and firm to the touch. Cool in the tins for 1 minute, then turn out and cool on a wire rack.

Cut the rind and all the white pith from the oranges, then cut into segments. To make the filling, chop half the orange segments, place in a bowl with the sugar and curd cheese and mix well together. Sandwich the cakes together with the filling. Arrange the remaining orange segments on the top and sprinkle with caster sugar.

▪ COOK'S TIP

If you would like a richer filling, substitute crème fraîche for the curd cheese and add 1 teaspoon orange Curaçao.

105 CRYSTALLIZED FRUIT CAKE

Preparation time:
35 minutes

Cooking time:
2½ hours

Oven temperature:
150C/300F/gas 2

**Makes 1 x 18 cm/
7 inch round cake**

Total calories:
3313

YOU WILL NEED:
175 g/6 oz butter
175 g/6 oz caster sugar
3 eggs, beaten
50 g/2 oz blanched almonds,
    chopped
50 g/2 oz glacé cherries
25 g/1 oz crystallized ginger,
    chopped
25 g/1 oz crystallized pineapple,
    chopped
50 g/2 oz dried apricots, chopped
50 g/2 oz ground almonds
175 g/6 oz plain flour
½ teaspoon baking powder
2 tablespoons apricot jam
50 g/2 oz mixed crystallized fruit,
    chopped

Put the butter and sugar in a bowl and beat until light and fluffy. Beat in the eggs a little at a time. Stir in the almonds, cherries, ginger, pineapple and apricots. Add the ground almonds. Sift the flour and baking powder into the bowl, then fold into the mixture with a metal spoon until evenly mixed.

Place in a greased and lined 18 cm/7 inch round cake tin and smooth the top. Bake for 2½ hours until the cake is light golden and springs back when pressed. Cool in the tin 30 minutes, turn out, remove the paper and cool on a wire rack.

Heat the jam with 1 tablespoon of water, add the chopped crystallized fruit and spread evenly over the top of the cake.

■ COOK'S TIP

*Make this rich moist cake
as an alternative to a
traditional Christmas cake,
which many people find too
heavy.*

106 SWISS ROLL

Preparation time:
15 minutes

Cooking time:
8-10 minutes

Oven temperature:
200C/400F/gas 6

Makes one Swiss Roll

Total calories:
972

YOU WILL NEED:
3 eggs
75 g/3 oz caster sugar
75 g/3 oz plain flour, sifted
caster sugar, to sprinkle
3 tablespoons strawberry or
    other jam

Grease and line a 33 x 23 cm/13 x 9 inch Swiss roll tin. Use the eggs, sugar and flour to make a Whisked sponge (see Introduction).

Put the mixture in the prepared tin. Shake the tin to level the mixture. Bake for 8-10 minutes, until light golden and firm to the touch.

Spread a piece of greaseproof paper on a work surface and sprinkle evenly with caster sugar. Turn the cake out on to the paper and remove the lining paper. Trim off the edges of the cake and spread quickly with the jam. Roll up from the short end using the sugared greaseproof paper to help you. Leave to cool.

■ COOK'S TIP

*Sweetened whipped cream,
flavoured with a liqueur,
can be used instead of jam
for a special occasion.*

107 ORANGE NUTFIELD CAKE

Preparation time:
50 minutes

Cooking time:
1-1¼ hours

Oven temperature:
180C/350F/gas 4

**Makes 1 x 18 cm/
7 inch square cake**

Total calories:
4131

YOU WILL NEED:
175 g/6 oz butter
225 g/8 oz caster sugar
4 eggs
75 g/3 oz plain flour, sifted
100 g/4 oz ground almonds
finely grated rind of 1 orange
1 tablespoon orange jelly
marmalade or apricot jam
finely grated rind of 1 orange
225 g/8 oz white marzipan

Cream the butter or margarine and sugar until very light, fluffy and pale. Beat in the eggs one at a time, following each with a spoonful of the flour. Fold in the remaining flour, then the ground almonds and orange rind. Turn into a greased and lined 18 cm/7 inch square tin and level the top.

Bake for just over 1 hour or until well risen, golden brown and firm to the touch. Cool in the tin for a minute or so before turning out on to a wire rack. Leave until cold; then peel off the paper. Brush the top with the marmalade or jam.

Knead the orange rind into the marzipan and roll out thinly to a square. Trim to fit the top of cake. Position the marzipan on the top of the cake. Roll the trimmings into long very thin sausages and lay on top of the cake from corner to corner, leaving about 4 cm/1½ inch between each one. Attach with a dab of jam if necessary and leave the marzipan to set.

COOK'S TIP

*If you do not like marzipan,
cover the cake with glacé
icing (see Introduction) and
scatter lightly toasted
almonds on top.*

108 SPICED SWISS ROULADE

Preparation time:
40 minutes

Cooking time:
15-20 minutes

Oven temperature:
190C/375F/gas 5

Makes one roll

Total calories:
3391

YOU WILL NEED:
4 eggs
100 g/4 oz caster sugar
100 g/4 oz plain flour, twice sifted
with ¼ teaspoon mixed spice and
½ teaspoon ground ginger
25 g/1 oz butter, melted
finely grated rind of ½ lemon
175-225 g/6-8 oz ginger preserve
1 quantity lemon Butter icing
(see Introduction)
FOR THE DECORATION
icing sugar
few pieces of stem ginger, sliced
few pieces of angelica, cut in strips

Use the eggs, sugar and flour to make a Whisked sponge (see Introduction), then fold in the cooled but still liquid butter. Turn quickly into a greased and lined 33 x 23 cm/13 x 9 inch Swiss roll tin, ensuring the corners are well filled. Bake for 15-20 minutes or until just firm to the touch. Turn out on to greaseproof paper lightly dredged with caster sugar. Peel off the paper, trim the edges and roll up the cake while still warm with the sugared paper inside. Cool on a wire rack.

Put a quarter of the butter icing into a piping bag with a star nozzle. Add the lemon rind to the remainder. Unroll the cake and remove the paper. Spread with ginger preserve, then with the butter and lemon icing. Re-roll the cake and dredge lightly with icing sugar. Pipe a row of whirls along the cake and decorate with stem ginger and angelica.

COOK'S TIP

*The easiest way to fill a
piping bag is to put it,
nozzle down, in a jug and
fold some of the bag over
the rim, thus leaving both
hands free.*

109 COCONUT-FROSTED MARBLE CAKE

Preparation time: about 30 minutes	YOU WILL NEED: *225 g/8 oz self-raising flour* *1½ teaspoons baking powder*
Cooking time: about 45 minutes	*175 g/6 oz caster sugar* *175 g/6 oz soft tub margarine* *3 eggs*
Oven temperature: 160C/325F/gas 3	*3 tablespoons milk* *grated rind of 1 lemon* *1 tablespoon cocoa powder, sifted*
Makes one medium ring cake	*1 quantity Seven-minute frosting (see Cook's tip)* *50 g/2 oz shredded coconut,*
Total calories: 4123	*toasted*

Grease a 1.1 litre/2 pint ring mould and dust the inside with flour. Sift the flour and baking powder into a bowl. Add the sugar, margarine, eggs and milk, and beat well for about 2 minutes until smooth and evenly blended. Put half the mixture into another bowl and beat in the lemon rind. Add the cocoa to the remaining mixture and beat until evenly distributed. Put alternate tablespoons of the mixtures into the ring mould to give a marbled effect. Level the top.

Bake for about 45 minutes or until well risen and firm to the touch. Cool for a minute or so in the mould, then turn out on to a wire rack and leave until cold. Swirl the frosting over the ring cake to cover it completely. Sprinkle quickly with the coconut as the icing tends to set quickly. Leave until set.

■ COOK'S TIP

Put 1 egg white, 150 g/5 oz caster sugar, a pinch of salt, 2 tablespoons water and a pinch of cream of tartar into a heatproof bowl and mix lightly. Stand over a *saucepan of simmering water and beat well, with a hand-held electric mixer, until thick enough to stand in peaks. Remove from the heat and use at once.*

110 PEANUT AND CRANBERRY CAKE

Preparation time: 20 minutes	YOU WILL NEED: *175 g/6 oz self-raising flour* *¾ teaspoon baking powder*
Cooking time: about 1 hour 10 minutes	*100 g/4 oz wholemeal flour* *100 g/4 oz butter or hard margarine* *100 g/4 oz light soft brown sugar* *grated rind of 1 lemon*
Oven temperature: 180C/350F/gas 4	*50 g/2 oz cut mixed peel* *100 g/4 oz cranberries, fresh or frozen and thawed, roughly*
Makes 1 x 23 x 13 cm/9 x 5 inch loaf	*chopped* *75 g/3 oz peanuts in kernels, shelled and roughly chopped*
Total calories: 3147	*2 eggs, beaten with 4 tablespoons milk*

Grease and line a 23 x 13 cm/9 x 5 inch loaf tin. Sift the self-raising flour and baking powder into a bowl and mix in the wholemeal flour. Add the butter or margarine and rub in until the mixture resembles fine breadcrumbs. Stir in the sugar, lemon rind, peel, cranberries and peanuts. Add the eggs and milk and mix to a fairly slack dough.

Turn into the tin, level the top roughly, and bake for about 1 hour 10 minutes or until cooked. Turn out on to a wire rack and leave to cool. Wrap in foil for 2 hours before cutting.

■ COOK'S TIP

Before buying unshelled peanuts, shake them. If you can hear the kernels rattling, it is a sign that the nuts are dried up.

111 ICED WALNUT CAKE

Preparation time:
40 minutes

Cooking time:
45-50 minutes

Oven temperature:
180C/350F/gas 4

**Makes 1 x 20 cm/
8 inch round cake**

Total calories:
3752

YOU WILL NEED:
175 g/6 oz butter, softened
175 g/6 oz light soft brown sugar
3 eggs
175 g/6 oz self-raising flour, sifted
1 tablespoon black treacle
50 g/2 oz shelled walnuts,
    chopped
icing (see Cook's Tip)
walnut halves, to decorate

Grease a 20 cm/8 inch round cake tin and line with greased greaseproof paper.

Cream the butter and sugar together until light and fluffy. Beat in the eggs one at a time, following each with a spoonful of flour. Fold in the remaining flour, followed by the black treacle and chopped walnuts. Turn into the prepared tin and level the top.

Bake in a preheated oven until well risen, golden brown and just firm to the touch. Turn out on to a wire rack and leave until cold, then strip off the paper.

Meanwhile, make the icing. Spread it quickly and evenly over the whole cake, using a round-bladed knife to swirl it attractively. Decorate the top of the cake with walnut halves and leave to set.

COOK'S TIP

Icing: put into a heatproof bowl set over a pan of simmering water 150 g/5 oz caster sugar, 1 egg white, 1 tablespoon water, 1 tablespoon coffee essence or *very strong black coffee and a good pinch of cream of tartar. Stir until the sugar has dissolved then whisk until the mixture stands in fairly stiff peaks.*

112 HARLEQUIN RING

Preparation time:
20-25 minutes

Cooking time:
40 minutes

Oven temperature:
180C/350F/gas 4

**Makes one large
ring cake**

Total calories:
4075

YOU WILL NEED:
175 g/6 oz butter or margarine
175 g/6 oz caster sugar
3 large eggs, beaten
175 g/6 oz self-raising flour
15 g/½ oz cocoa powder,
    dissolved in 3 tablespoons milk
grated rind of ½ lemon
1 tablespoon lemon juice
yellow food colouring
FOR THE TOPPING
225 g/8 oz granulated sugar
4 tablespoons water
1 egg white
5 g/2 oz long-thread coconut,
    toasted

Cream the fat and sugar until light and fluffy. Add the eggs with a little flour and beat well. Fold in the remaining flour. Remove two-thirds of the mixture and mix with the cocoa. Add the lemon rind, juice and colouring to the remaining mixture. Spread the cocoa mixture over the bottom and sides of a greased 1.75 litre/3 pint ring mould. Place the lemon mixture in a piping bag with a large plain nozzle and pipe around the centre of the chocolate mixture. Using a palette knife, level the surface. Bake 40 minutes, cool on a wire rack.

To make the topping, dissolve the sugar in the water, then boil to 115C/240F or the soft ball stage. Whisk the egg white until stiff. Pour the sugar syrup over and whisk until opaque. Swirl quickly over the cake and sprinkle with coconut.

COOK'S TIP

If you do not have a sugar thermometer, you can test a syrup for the soft ball stage by dropping some of it into a bowl of iced water. The syrup should form a soft *ball when squeezed between the fingers.*

Small Cakes & Patisserie

The irresistible small cakes and pastries in this chapter make perfect teatime treats. Many of them are also ideal for serving at parties and as desserts. You will find a variety of pastry doughs used in many of the recipes. There are also numerous toppings and icings, which could be used on large cakes as well as small ones.

Cheese and Honey Tartlets

113 RASPBERRY VOL-AU-VENTS

Preparation time:
about 25-50 minutes

Cooking time:
about 25 minutes

Oven temperature:
220C/425F/gas 7

Makes 8

Calories:
413 per portion

YOU WILL NEED:
8 large individual frozen or ready-baked vol-au-vents; or 450 g/ 1 lb puff pastry
beaten egg, to glaze
1 x recipe quantity Crème patissière (see Introduction)
1-2 tablespoons Amaretto di Saronno; or the finely grated rind of 1 lemon
175 g/6 oz raspberries
about 5 tablespoons double or whipping cream, whipped

Cook frozen vol-au-vents following the instructions on the packet. If using puff pastry, roll out to about 1 cm/⅓-½ inch thickness and cut out 8 x 7.5 cm/3 inch vol-au-vents. Use a smaller cutter to cut part way through the centre of the pastry round, leaving an even margin. Stand on a greased baking sheet and glaze with beaten egg. Bake in a preheated oven for 20-25 minutes, turning the sheet round in the oven once, until well risen, golden brown and firm. Take the soft pastry from the centre and discard. Cool the vol-au-vents on a wire tray.

Make the crème patissière; in place of the vanilla essence beat in the Amaretto liqueur or the lemon rind. Cover and leave until cold. Use to fill the vol-au-vents. Reserve 8 of the best raspberries and arrange the remainder over the tops of the vol-au-vents. Pipe a whirl of cream on top of the raspberries and top with the reserved raspberries.

■ COOK'S TIP

Other seedless fruits, such as peaches, strawberries, mandarins, melons cut into dice or balls, grapes etc. can be used in place of the raspberries. The fruits can *be soaked in a little of the Amaretto di Saronno for a couple of hours.*

114 CHEESE AND HONEY TARTLETS

Preparation time:
about 45 minutes,

Cooking time:
about 20 minutes

Oven temperature:
190C/375F/gas 5

Makes 8

Calories:
506 per portion

YOU WILL NEED:
1 x recipe quantity Pâte sucrée (see Cook's Tip, recipe 231)
225 g/8 oz full fat soft cheese
3 tablespoons clear honey
grated rind of ½ orange
a good pinch of ground cinnamon
150 ml/¼ pint whipping cream, whipped until stiff
FOR THE TOPPING
225 g/8 oz blackcurrants
4-6 tablespoons water
sugar to taste

Roll out the pastry and line 8 9-10 cm/3½-4 inch individual flan tins. Bake blind in a preheated oven for about 10 minutes; remove the beans and paper and return to the oven to dry out for a few minutes. Cool on a wire tray. Roll out the pastry trimmings and cut into 8 or 16 leaf shapes about 2.5 cm/1 inch long. Bake on a lightly greased baking sheet in a preheated oven for about 7 minutes until lightly browned.

Put the blackcurrants in a pan with the water, cover and cook gently until tender. Sweeten to taste and leave to cool.

Beat the cheese until smooth then beat in the honey, orange rind, and cinnamon. Fold in a third of the cream. Divide the mixture between the pastry cases. Spoon over the blackcurrant mixture. Put the remaining cream into a piping bag with a star nozzle and use it and the pastry leaves to decorate the tartlets.

■ COOK'S TIP

Cranberries, either fresh or frozen and thawed, make a good alternative fruit to the blackcurrants in these tartlets.

115 STRAWBERRY PALMIERS

Preparation time:
20-25 minutes

Cooking time:
20 minutes

Oven temperature:
220C/425F/gas 7

Makes 8

Calories:
550 per palmier

YOU WILL NEED:
150 g/5 oz caster sugar
1 x 368 g/13 oz packet frozen puff
  pastry, defrosted
225 g/8 oz strawberries
450 ml/¾ pint double cream
2 teaspoons icing sugar, sifted

Sprinkle a board with 25 g/1 oz of the sugar and roll out the pastry to a 30 cm/12 inch square. Trim the edges of the square, brush with water and sprinkle with 50 g/2 oz of the sugar. Fold two opposite sides together to meet in the centre, brush again with water and sprinkle with the remaining sugar. Fold again in the same way and press down lightly. Finally, fold the two sides up together to produce a single roll that when cut across will form heart-shaped slices. Cut into 16 1 cm/½ inch slices and place on a baking tray.

Bake for 10 minutes, turn over with a spatula and bake for a further 10 minutes. Cool on a wire rack.

Halve the strawberries and reserve a few to decorate. Whip the cream with the sugar until thick. Sandwich the palmiers with the cream and strawberries. Decorate the tops with the reserved strawberries.

116 CHESTNUT TULIPS

Preparation time:
30 minutes

Cooking time:
about 20 minutes

Oven temperature:
200C/400F/gas 6

Makes 8

Calories:
296 per portion

YOU WILL NEED:
FOR THE TULIP BASKETS:
40 g/1½ oz plain flour, sifted
75 g/3 oz caster sugar
3 egg whites
25 g/1 oz butter, melted
FOR THE CHESTNUT CREAM
100 g/4 oz plain chocolate, chopped
150 ml/¼ pint double cream
1 x 227 g/8 oz can unsweetened
  chestnut purée
1 tablespoon caster sugar
2 tablespoons brandy
8 chocolate triangles, to decorate

Mix the flour and sugar in a bowl. Add the egg whites and butter and beat until smooth. Place 3 tablespoons of this mixture on a greased baking tray and spread to form a 13 cm/5 inch round. Repeat with another 3 tablespoons of the mixture.

Bake for 4-5 minutes, until golden. Leave to cool slightly, then remove with a plastic spatula and place each one top side down over the base of an inverted and oiled glass, moulding to give wavy edges. Leave to set. Repeat with the remaining mixture to make a total of 8.

For the filling, heat the chocolate and cream in a pan until melted, then cool. Blend the chestnut purée, sugar, chocolate and brandy in a blender or food processor until smooth. Pipe into the tulip cases. Decorate with chocolate triangles.

■ COOK'S TIP

Unfilled palmiers will keep fresh in an airtight tin for several days. Fill at the last moment to appreciate the crisp pastry and creamy filling.

■ COOK'S TIP

Chocolate triangles: spread a thin layer of melted chocolate on to greaseproof paper. Leave until just set. Cut into squares, then triangles. Carefully lift the *tip of the paper and peel away the thin triangles of chocolate.*

117 CHOCOLATE ECLAIRS

Preparation time:
30 minutes

Cooking time:
30-35 minutes

Oven temperature:
220C/425F/gas 7;
then 190C/375F/gas 5

Makes 8

Calories:
257 per portion

YOU WILL NEED:
½ x recipe quantity Choux pastry
   (see Introduction)
FOR THE FILLING AND TOPPING
150 ml/¼ pint double or whipping
   cream
100 g/4 oz plain chocolate

Make the Choux pastry according to the instructions in the Introduction to this book.

Place the choux pastry in a piping bag fitted with a large plain tube. Pipe about eight 10 cm/4 inch lengths, well apart, on to a greased baking sheet. Bake in a preheated oven for 10 minutes, then reduce the heat and cook for a further 20-25 minutes, until the eclairs are crisp and golden. Place on a wire tray and pierce the sides with a knife. This will allow the steam to escape and prevent the eclairs from becoming soggy.

Whip the cream until thick, and use to fill the cold eclairs.

Melt the chocolate in a bowl over a saucepan of hot water. Dip the top of each eclair into the chocolate to coat.

■ COOK'S TIP

This mixture will make about 12 choux buns, which should be put in spoonfuls on the baking sheet. Bake as for eclairs.

118 MOCHA BOXES

Preparation time:
about 1½ hours

Cooking time:
about 50 minutes

Oven temperature:
190C/375F/gas 5

Makes 16

Calories: 218 each

YOU WILL NEED:
1 recipe quantity coffee-flavoured
   Victoria sandwich (recipe 93)
2 x recipe quantities Butter cream
   (see Introduction) flavoured
   with 3-4 teaspoons rum
about 225 g/8 oz plain or cake
   covering chocolate

Bake the cake mixture in a greased and lined 20 cm/8 inch deep square cake tin for 50 minutes, until well risen and firm to the touch. Cool in the tin for a minute then turn out on to a wire tray. Leave until cold. Remove the paper and cut the cake into 5 cm/2 inch squares. Make up the butter cream and flavour with rum.

Melt the chocolate and spread out thinly on non-stick paper. When beginning to set mark into 80 pieces measuring 5 cm/2 inch wide by the height of the cake. Mark with a knife and a ruler and leave to set. When dry, peel off the paper.

Scrape up the chocolate trimmings, melt and spread out on non-stick paper. As it dries, cut it into 16 x 4 cm/1½ inch squares and then cut in half to make triangles. Spread the sides of the cakes with butter cream and stick 5 side pieces around each. Put the remaining butter cream into a piping bag with a star nozzle and pipe a large whirl on top of each box. Add 2 triangles of chocolate to each for decoration. Leave to set.

■ COOK'S TIP

Mocha is a strongly-flavoured coffee from Mocha in Arabia. The word is used in cookery for cakes flavoured with coffee and sometimes for a mixture of coffee and chocolate.

119 CHERRY TARTLETS

Preparation time:	YOU WILL NEED:
about 45 minutes	*100 g/4 oz plain flour*
	pinch of salt
Cooking time:	*50 g/2 oz plain wholewheat flour*
about 25 minutes	*40 g/1½ oz butter*
	40 g/1½ oz lard or white fat
Oven temperature:	*cold water to mix*
200C/400F/gas 6	*100 g/4 oz redcurrant jelly*
	100 g/4 oz glacé cherries
Makes 6	*½ recipe quantity Victoria*
	sandwich mixture (recipe 93)
Calories:	*few drops almond essence*
549 per portion	*lemon icing, to decorate*
	25 g/1 oz blanched almonds,
	chopped and toasted

Warm a baking sheet in a preheated oven. For the pastry: sift the plain flour and salt into a bowl then mix in the wholewheat flour. Add the fats and rub in until the mixture resembles fine breadcrumbs. Add sufficient cold water to mix to a pliable dough. Knead the dough until smooth, then roll out and use to line 6 individual flan tins 10-11 cm/4-4½ inches in diameter.

Spread a thin layer of jelly in the base of each. Reserve 6 cherries, slice the rest and divide between the pastry cases. Add a few drops of almond essence to the Victoria sandwich mixture and divide between the pastry cases. Stand the tins on the hot baking sheet and bake in a preheated oven 25 minutes or until golden brown and firm. Remove from the tins and cool on a wire tray. Spread the icing over the tartlets. Add a cherry to each and sprinkle with toasted nuts. Leave to set.

▪ COOK'S TIP

To make lemon icing, blend 100 g/4 oz sifted icing sugar with lemon juice (1 - 2 tablespoons) to make a smooth thick icing.

120 PEACH FRANGIPAN TARTS

Preparation time:	YOU WILL NEED:
about 45 minutes,	*1 recipe quantity Crème patissière*
plus chilling and	*(see Introduction)*
standing	*40 g/1½ oz ground almonds*
	a few drops of almond essence
Cooking time:	*1-2 tablespoons cream or top of*
about 15 minutes	*the milk*
	8 baked Pâte sucrée tartlet cases
Oven temperature:	*(see Cheese and honey tartlets,*
190C/375F/gas 5	*recipe 114)*
	1 x 425 g/15 oz can sliced peaches
Makes 8	*(see Cook's Tip)*
	3 tablespoons brandy
Calories:	*2 teaspoons arrowroot*
502 per portion	*a few blanched pistachio nuts*

Make up the crème patissière and then beat in the ground almonds, essence and sufficient cream or milk until thick but not too stodgy. Cover with cling film and leave until cold.

To assemble, fill the pastry cases evenly with the custard.

Drain the peaches, reserve the liquid, slice the fruit evenly (if whole pieces) and use to arrange over the custard.

Thicken 150 ml/¼ pint of the peach liquid with the arrowroot, bringing to the boil until clear. Cool slightly, the brush or spoon over to coat the peaches. Leave until cold.

Before serving, decorate with pistachio nuts.

▪ COOK'S TIP

To use canned peaches, drain off half the juice and put the remaining juice and the peaches into a bowl with the 3 tablespoons brandy. Cover and leave to stand for 24 hours, stirring occasionally before use.

121 BUTTERFLY CAKES

Preparation time:
about 40 minutes

Cooking time:
about 20 minutes

Oven temperature:
190C/375F/gas 5

Makes 16

Calories:
213 per portion

YOU WILL NEED:
*1 Victoria sandwich cake mixture
  using 100 g/4 oz each of butter or
  margarine, sugar, flour and 2
  eggs (recipe 93), flavoured as below*
*1 x recipe Butter cream
  (Introduction), coloured and
  flavoured to blend with the cake
icing sugar, for dredging
  (optional)*

Line 16 patty tins with paper cases or grease them thoroughly. Make up the cake mixture using either coffee, chocolate, lemon, orange or vanilla for flavouring. Divide between the paper cases or patty tins. Place in a preheated oven and bake for about 15-20 minutes or until well risen and just firm to the touch. Turn out on to a wire tray and leave to cool.

Make up and flavour the butter cream.

Cut a small piece out of the top of each bun, leaving about 1 cm/½ inch all round the top surface uncut; and cut this piece in half to form the 'wings'.

Put the butter cream into a piping bag fitted with a star nozzle and pipe a whirl to fill up the hole which has been cut out. Place the 'wings' in position, tilting them up at the edges and either leave as they are or pipe a little more butter cream between and round the wings.

Dredge lightly with icing sugar and serve.

■ COOK'S TIP

*For a luxury alternative, use
thickly whipped double
cream instead of the butter
cream.*

122 TRAY BAKE FINGERS

Preparation time:
about 1 hour

Cooking time:
40-45 minutes

Oven temperature:
160C/325F/gas 3

Makes 14-16

Calories:
370-324 per portion

YOU WILL NEED:
*150 g/6 oz self-raising flour
1½ teaspoons baking powder
150 g/6 oz soft tub margarine
150 g/6 oz caster sugar
3 large eggs
2 tablespoons sifted cocoa
  blended with 2 tablespoons hot
  water
1½ x recipe quantities chocolate
Butter cream (see Introduction)
DECORATION (A SELECTION OF):
glacé cherries
chopped toasted nuts
chocolate buttons
angelica*

Grease and line a rectangular tin about 28 x 18 x 4 cm/11 x 7 x 1½ inch. Sift the flour and baking powder into a bowl and add the margarine, sugar, eggs and cocoa mixture. Beat until smooth and evenly blended.

Turn the mixture into the tin, making sure there is plenty in the corners, and bake in a preheated oven for 40-45 minutes or until well risen and firm to the touch. Turn out on to a wire tray and leave until cold, then peel off the paper.

Make up the butter cream. Spread a thinnish layer over the top of the cake. Put the remainder into a piping bag with a star nozzle. Decorate the top of the icing with piping. Add chosen decorations and leave to set. Cut first down the centre and then cut each bar into fingers between the decorations.

■ COOK'S TIP

*Instead of the cocoa
mixture, sift 1½
tablespoons instant coffee
powder into the flour; use a
coffee butter cream to ice
the cake. Alternatively, use*

*½ teaspoon almond essence
instead of the chocolate or
coffee.*

123 LEMON MAIDS

Preparation time:	YOU WILL NEED:
20-25 minutes	*225 g/8 oz plain flour*
	100 g/4 oz butter or margarine
Cooking time:	*grated rind of 2 lemons*
20 minutes	*40 g/1½ oz caster sugar*
	1 tablespoon cold water
Oven temperature:	*4 tablespoons lemon curd*
180C/350F/gas 4	*FOR THE SPONGE TOPPING*
	75 g/3 oz butter, softened
Makes 18	*75 g/3 oz caster sugar*
	75 g/3 oz self-raising flour
Calories:	*25 g/1 oz ground almonds*
225 per portion	*1 egg, lightly beaten*
	3 tablespoons lemon juice
	FOR THE ICING
	175 g/6 oz lemon curd
	75 g/3 oz ground almonds
	coarsely grated lemon rind

To make the pastry, sift the flour into a bowl, rub in the butter, then add the lemon rind and sugar. Add the water and mix to a smooth dough. Roll out thinly and cut out 18 6-7.5 cm/2½-3 inch rounds and use to line patty tins. Place a little lemon curd in each case.

To make the sponge topping, place all the ingredients in a bowl and beat until pale and fluffy. Spoon over the lemon curd. Bake for 20 minutes, until well risen and golden. Turn out to cool on a wire rack.

To ice the cakes, mix the lemon curd and ground almonds and spread over the cooled cakes. Decorate with lemon rind.

▦ COOK'S TIP

These cakes can also be made with an orange flavouring. Use the grated rind of 1 large orange and 4 tablespoons orange curd for the bases; 3 tablespoons *orange juice for the sponge topping; and 175 g/6 oz orange curd with grated orange rind for the decoration.*

124 ST CATHERINE'S CAKES

Preparation time:	YOU WILL NEED:
20 minutes	*350 g/12 oz plain flour*
	½ teaspoon bicarbonate of soda
Cooking time:	*1 teaspoon mixed spice*
12-15 minutes	*25 g/1 oz ground almonds*
	225 g/8 oz caster sugar
Oven temperature:	*225 g/8 oz butter or margarine*
200C/400F/gas 6	*50 g/2 oz currants*
	1 egg, lightly beaten
Makes 24	*25 g/1 oz granulated sugar*

Calories:
174 per portion

Sift the flour, bicarbonate of soda and spice into a bowl. Stir in the almonds and caster sugar.

Add the butter or margarine, cut into pieces, and rub in until the mixture resembles fine breadcrumbs. Stir in the currants.

Add the beaten egg and mix to a firm dough. Turn out on to a floured surface and knead lightly.

Roll out the dough to an oblong 30 x 20 cm/12 x 8 inch. Brush with water and sprinkle with the granulated sugar. Cut into strips 1 x 20 cm/½ x 8 inch.

Form each strip into a coil, then place on greased baking sheets, leaving room for each coil to spread.

Bake in a preheated oven for 12-15 minutes, until light golden. Cool slightly, then remove from the baking sheet and finish cooling on a wire tray. Serve warm or cold.

▦ COOK'S TIP

Mixed spice is a mixture of cloves, cinnamon, nutmeg and sometimes coriander and allspice. Buy it in small quantities as it soon loses its strength.

125 RASPBERRY VIENNESE SWIRLS

Preparation time:	YOU WILL NEED:
20 minutes	225 g/8 oz butter, softened
	50 g/2 oz icing sugar, sifted
Cooking time:	¼ teaspoon vanilla essence
20-25 minutes	225 g/8 oz plain flour
	50 g/2 oz cornflour
Oven temperature:	icing sugar, to dust
180C/350F/gas 4	2 tablespoons seedless raspberry
	jam
Makes 12	

Calories:
246 per portion

Cream the butter with the sugar until light and fluffy. Beat in the vanilla essence. Sift the flour with the cornflour and gradually beat into the creamed mixture. Place in a piping bag fitted with a large star-shaped nozzle. Pipe swirls of the mixture into 12 paper bun cases set in bun tins.

Bake for 20-25 minutes or until light golden brown. Cool on a wire rack.

Dust the tops with icing sugar and place a small spoonful of jam in the centre of each.

126 COFFEE KISSES

Preparation time:	YOU WILL NEED:
20 minutes	100 g/4 oz butter or margarine
	50 g/2 oz caster sugar
Cooking time:	125 g/5 oz self-raising flour
10 minutes	3 tablespoons strong black coffee
	FOR THE ICING
Oven temperature:	50 g/2 oz butter, softened
190C/375F/gas 5	100 g/4 oz icing sugar, sifted
	1 tablespoon strong black coffee
Makes about 15	icing sugar, for dusting

Calories:
161 per portion

Lightly grease a baking sheet.

Place the butter or margarine and sugar in a bowl. Beat until light and fluffy. Add the flour and coffee and mix to a stiff dough.

Place the mixture in a piping bag fitted with a large star nozzle. Pipe an even number of small stars of the mixture, a little apart, on the baking sheet. The mixture will make about 30 stars.

Bake in a preheated oven for 10 minutes, until just beginning to colour. Cool on the baking sheet for 5 minutes, then remove and leave to cool completely on a wire tray.

To make the icing, beat together the butter, icing sugar and coffee until light and creamy.

Sandwich 2 stars together with a little icing, then dust with icing sugar.

■ COOK'S TIP

If you heat the jam a little first before spooning into the centre of the swirls you will achieve a more professional finish.

■ COOK'S TIP

Soften the butter by putting it in a bowl and standing the bowl in warm water for a minute or two. Do not let the butter become oily.

127 CHOCOLATE CUP CAKES

Preparation time:
20 minutes

Cooking time:
12-15 minutes

Oven temperature:
190C/375F/gas 5

Makes 24

Calories:
104 per portion

YOU WILL NEED:
100 g/4 oz butter or margarine
100 g/4 oz caster sugar
2 eggs, beaten
2 tablespoons cocoa
2 tablespoons boiling water
100 g/4 oz self-raising flour
100 g/4 oz plain chocolate

Place the butter or margarine and sugar in a bowl. Beat with a wooden spoon for 10 minutes or in a mixer for 5 minutes, until light and fluffy. Beat in the eggs, a little at a time.

Blend the cocoa and boiling water to a smooth paste, then beat into the cake mixture. Add the flour and fold in lightly with a metal spoon.

Line a bun tin with paper cake cases and put teaspoonfuls of the mixture in each. Do not overfill. Bake in a preheated oven for 12-15 minutes, until firm to the touch. Leave to cool.

Break the chocolate into a bowl over a saucepan of hot water, until the chocolate has melted. Spread a layer of chocolate evenly over each cake. Leave to set.

COOK'S TIP

Use plain dark chocolate for the icing, not the chocolate cake covering available in slabs from the baking ingredients shelves of the supermarket.

128 CHOCOLATE TOFFEE BARS

Preparation time:
25 minutes, plus cooling

Cooking time:
35 minutes

Oven temperature:
160C/325F/gas 3

Makes 24

Calories:
199 per portion

YOU WILL NEED:
175 g/6 oz butter
75 g/3 oz caster sugar
250 g/9 oz plain flour
FOR THE TOPPING
100 g/4 oz butter
50 g/2 oz caster sugar
2 tablespoons golden syrup
1 x 200 g/7 oz can condensed milk
100 g/4 oz plain or milk chocolate

To make the cake, place the butter and sugar in a bowl. Beat until light and fluffy. Add the flour and mix to a soft dough. Knead the dough lightly on a floured surface, then roll out and line an 18 x 28 cm/7 x 11 inch shallow oblong tin.

Bake in a preheated oven for 35 minutes, until just beginning to colour. Leave to cool in the tin.

To make the topping, place the butter, sugar, syrup and condensed milk in a heavy-based saucepan. Heat gently until the sugar has dissolved, then boil for 5 minutes, stirring until toffee-coloured and thickened. Cool slightly, then spread over the cake. Leave until cold.

Break up the chocolate and place in a bowl over a saucepan of hot water until it has melted. Spread the chocolate evenly over the toffee, making wavy lines with a round-ended knife. Leave to set, then cut into 3 lengthways and 8 across.

COOK'S TIP

If you find the shortbread mixture difficult to roll out, then simply press the dough evenly into the tin using the back of a tablespoon or your fingers.

129 CRUNCHY FRUIT BARS

Preparation time:	YOU WILL NEED:
15 minutes	225 g/8 oz dried fruit salad
	(e.g. peaches, pears, apples,
Cooking time:	bananas, dates, figs), chopped
about 1 hour	300 ml/½ pint water
	150 ml/¼ pint orange juice
Oven temperature:	150 g/6 oz plain flour
190C/375F/gas 5	100 g/4 oz semolina
	100 g/4 oz butter or margarine
Makes 16	75 g/3 oz caster sugar
	granulated sugar, for sprinkling
Calories:	
166 per portion	

Place the dried fruit, water and orange juice in a saucepan. Bring to the boil, then reduce the heat, cover and cook gently for 30 minutes. Leave to cool.

Place the flour and semolina in a bowl. Add the butter or margarine, cut into pieces, and rub in until the mixture resembles fine breadcrumbs. Stir in the caster sugar.

Sprinkle half the crumble evenly over the base of a 28 x 18 cm/11 x 7 inch shallow tin. Carefully spread the fruit over the top and sprinkle with the remaining crumble. Press down lightly.

Bake in a preheated oven for 30-35 minutes, until pale golden. Sprinkle with granulated sugar and leave in the tin until cold. Cut in half down the length, then into 8 across to make into bars.

130 APPLE AND GINGER RINGS

Preparation time:	YOU WILL NEED:
15-20 minutes	2 eggs
	100 g/4 oz golden syrup
Cooking time:	1 medium cooking apple, about
20-25 minutes	175 g/6 oz
	juice of 1 lemon
Oven temperature:	1 piece preserved ginger, chopped
190C/375F/gas 5	100 g/4 oz self-raising flour
	¼ teaspoon ground ginger
Makes 9	FOR THE ICING AND
	DECORATION
Calories:	100 g/4 oz icing sugar
163 per ring	1-2 tablespoons ginger wine
	crystallized ginger
	few slices of apple, dipped in
	lemon juice

Whisk the eggs with the syrup until pale and thick. Peel, core and grate the apple, sprinkle with the lemon juice and mix with the preserved ginger. Fold the apple mixture into the eggs. Sift the flour with the ground ginger and fold into the egg mixture. Divide the mixture between nine well-greased 11 cm/4½ inch ring tins. Bake for 20-25 minutes then turn out to cool on a wire rack.

To ice rings, sift the icing sugar into a bowl and mix to a smooth consistency with the ginger wine. Drizzle the icing over the cooled cakes and decorate with crystallized ginger and small pieces of apple.

■ COOK'S TIP

Try replacing the dried fruit salad with chopped dates and add the rind and juice of 1 lemon.

■ COOK'S TIP

To prevent fruit from discolouring, slice with a stainless steel knife and sprinkle with lemon juice.

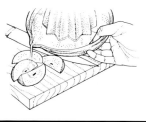

131 AMERICAN APPLE CAKES

Preparation time:
20 minutes

Cooking time:
1¾ hours

Oven temperature:
180C/350F/gas 4
then 150C/300F/gas 2

Makes 24

Calories:
168 per portion

YOU WILL NEED:
100 g/4 oz butter
350 g/12 oz caster sugar
2 eggs, beaten
225 g/8 oz plain flour
1 teaspoon bicarbonate of soda
1½ teaspoons ground cinnamon
1½ teaspoons grated nutmeg
pinch of salt
675 g/1½ lb dessert apples, peeled,
    cored and finely chopped
100 g/4 oz chopped mixed nuts

Cream the butter and sugar together until light and fluffy. Gradually beat in the eggs, mixing well. Sift the flour, soda, spices and salt together and fold into the creamed mixture, then fold in the apples and nuts. Turn into a greased 23 x 33 cm/9 x 13 inch tin.

Bake for 1¼ hours at the higher temperature, then lower the temperature and cook for a further 45 minutes. Cool in the tin, then turn out and cut into squares.

132 CHERRY BUMPERS

Preparation time:
25 minutes, plus
cooling

Cooking time:
20-25 minutes

Oven temperature:
200C/400F/gas 6

Makes 12

Calories:
119 per portion

YOU WILL NEED:
350 g/12 oz cherries, stoned
50 g/2 oz sugar
1 tablespoon water
200 g/8 oz Shortcrust pastry
    (see Introduction)
milk, to glaze

Place the cherries, sugar and water in a saucepan. Cook gently, stirring occasionally, until the cherries are softened (about 5 minutes). Leave to cool.

Roll out the pastry and cut into twelve 10 cm/4 inch rounds. Divide the cherries between the rounds and damp the edges of the pastry.

Draw up the pastry over the filling, pressing the edges to seal. Flute the join by pinching with the fingers.

Place the bumpers on a baking sheet and brush with milk. Bake in a preheated oven for 20-25 minutes until golden brown. Serve warm or cold.

▪ COOK'S TIP

This rich, moist apple cake can be frozen. Cut into squares then freeze for up to 3 months in a rigid container. Defrost at room temperature for about 2-3 hours.

▪ COOK'S TIP

For apple and sultana bumpers, peel, core and chop 1 large cooking apple. Cook with 50 g/2 oz sugar and 3 tablespoons water until soft. Stir in 25 g/1 oz *sultanas and use the mixture as in the recipe.*

133 COCONUT MERINGUE SLICES

Preparation time:
20 minutes

Cooking time:
30 minutes

Oven temperature:
180C/350F/gas 4

Makes 14

Calories:
130 per portion

YOU WILL NEED:
200 g/8 oz Shortcrust pastry
(see Introduction)
3 tablespoons raspberry jam
2 large egg whites
100 g/4 oz caster sugar
100 g/4 oz desiccated coconut

Grease an 18 x 28 cm/7 x 11 inch Swiss roll tin. Roll out the pastry and use to line the bottom of the tin. Spread with the jam.

Whisk the egg whites until they stand in stiff peaks. Gradually whisk in half the sugar a teaspoonful at a time. Fold in the remaining sugar and most of the coconut. Spoon on top of the jam and spread carefully with a palette knife.

Bake in a moderate oven for about 15 minutes. Sprinkle with the remaining coconut and return to the oven until the top is golden. Allow to cool in the tin and cut into fingers while still warm.

134 SPICED CURD TARTS

Preparation time:
15 minutes

Cooking time:
30 minutes

Oven temperature:
180C/350F/gas 4

Makes 14-16

Calories:
170-149 per portion

YOU WILL NEED:
1 x recipe Shortcrust pastry
(see Introduction)
50 g/2 oz stoned or seedless raisins
50 g/2 oz butter
50 g/2 oz caster sugar
1 teaspoon finely grated lemon rind
1 large egg, lightly beaten
1 tablespoon self-raising flour
½ teaspoon ground cinnamon
200 g/8 oz curd cheese
2 tablespoons milk

Roll out the pastry, cut into 8 cm/3 inch circles with a fluted cutter and use to line 14-16 patty tins. Lightly prick the pastry and put a few raisins in the bottom of each tart.

Cream the butter, sugar and lemon rind until soft and light. Gradually beat in the egg, then the flour sieved with the cinnamon, the cheese and the milk. Divide the mixture between the pastry cases. Bake in a moderate oven for about 30 minutes or until the filling is well risen and set.

▪ COOK'S TIP

If you don't care for the seeds in raspberry jam, use apricot or black cherry jam instead.

▪ COOK'S TIP

Curd cheese is a very simple cheese, made by heating milk, plus an acid such as lemon juice, very slowly until a curd forms. The whey is then drained off, *usually through cheesecloth.*

135 HEAVENLY FAVOURS

Preparation time:	YOU WILL NEED:
25 minutes, plus	*FOR THE DOUGH*
resting the dough	*200 g/8 oz plain flour*
	¼ teaspoon salt
Cooking time:	*25 g/1 oz lard*
about 3-5 minutes	*25 g/1 oz margarine*
	2 large eggs, lightly beaten
Makes about 18	*1-2 tablespoons milk*
	deep oil or fat, for frying
Calories:	*caster sugar*
86 per portion	*ground cinnamon*

Sift the flour and salt. Rub in the lard and margarine. Add the eggs and milk and mix to a soft dough. Turn on to a lightly-floured surface and knead for about 5 minutes until the mixture is smooth. Cover and leave in a warm place for 1 hour.

Place the dough on a floured surface and roll out to a rectangle. Fold the top third down and the bottom third up like an envelope, and give the dough a half turn. Repeat this twice and leave the dough to rest for 10 minutes. Roll out the dough until it is 6 mm/¼ inch thick and cut it into diamonds.

Heat the fat until a cube of bread browns in 40-50 seconds and fry the pastry diamonds until they are golden brown. Remove from the fat and drain, sprinkle with sugar and cinnamon and serve while still warm.

██ COOK'S TIP

These fried pastries are delicious served with jam: try apricot, plum or cherry jams.

136 FRUIT-FILLED BOATS

Preparation time:	YOU WILL NEED:
25 minutes	*FOR THE PASTRY*
	150 g/6 oz plain flour
Cooking time:	*pinch of salt*
10 minutes	*75 g/3 oz butter or margarine*
	25 g/1 oz caster sugar
Oven temperature:	*1 large egg yolk*
190C/375F/gas 5	*a very little water*
	FOR THE FILLING
Makes 12	*200 g/8 oz fresh or canned fruit*
	4 tablespoons redcurrant jelly
Calories:	*1 tablespoon fruit juice*
169 per portion	*125 ml/¼ pint double cream,*
	lightly whipped

Sift together the flour and salt. Rub in the butter or margarine until the mixture resembles fine breadcrumbs. Add the sugar and bind with the egg yolk and water to a stiff dough. Turn on to a floured surface and knead very lightly.

Use the pastry to line 12 boat tins about 10 x 5 cm/4 x 2 inch. Prick the sides and bases and bake blind in a moderately hot oven for 10 minutes. Allow to cool and remove from the tins.

Arrange the fruit attractively in the pastry cases. Melt the jelly with the fruit juice over a very low heat and brush over the fruit; if you are using an orange fruit, such as mandarins, you may prefer to use sieved apricot jam. Leave until the glaze is quite cold. Spoon the cream into a piping bag with a small rose nozzle and use to decorate the boats.

██ COOK'S TIP

Fruits to choose from include cherries, strawberries, raspberries, gooseberries and mandarins.

137 MACAROON MINCEMEAT TARTS

Preparation time:
25 minutes

Cooking time:
20 minutes

Oven temperature:
190C/375F/gas 5

Makes 10-12

Calories:
169-140 per portion

YOU WILL NEED:
150 g/6 oz shortcrust pastry
4 tablespoons mincemeat
2 large egg whites
75 g/3 oz caster sugar
75 g/3 oz ground almonds
15 g/½ oz flaked almonds
few glacé cherries, quartered

Roll out the pastry, cut into 8 cm/3 inch circles and use to line 10-12 patty tins. Divide the mincemeat between the pastry cases.

Whisk the egg whites until they are stiff. Fold in the sugar and almonds. Pile the macaroon mixture on top of the mincemeat and sprinkle with the flaked almonds. Place a quartered cherry in the centre of each tart. Bake in a moderately hot oven for 20 minutes or until golden brown.

138 BALMORAL TARTS

Preparation time:
20 minutes

Cooking time:
about 20 minutes

Oven temperature:
190C/375F/gas 5

Makes 8

Calories:
263 per portion

YOU WILL NEED:
½ x recipe Rich shortcrust
pastry (see Introduction)
50 g/2 oz butter
50 g/2 oz caster sugar
1 egg, separated
25 g/1 oz cake crumbs
15 g/½ oz glacé cherries, chopped
15 g/½ oz mixed chopped peel
½ teaspoon cornflour
1 teaspoon brandy, optional
sieved icing sugar, to finish

Grease eight patty tins. Roll out the pastry thinly, just under 5 mm/¼ inch thick. Cut out 8 rounds about 2.5 cm/1 inch larger than the top of the patty pans, using a fluted cutter. Line the patty tins with the pastry and prick the bases with a fork. Place them on a baking sheet.

Soften the butter, beat in the sugar and when creamy beat in the egg yolk. Stir in the crumbs, chopped cherries and peel and the cornflour and mix well with the brandy, if used. Whisk the egg white until stiff but still moist, and fold into the mixture. Fill the pastry cases with the mixture.

Bake in a preheated oven for 20 minutes, or until set and golden. Allow the tarts to shrink slightly before lifting out on to a wire tray to cool. When cold, sift icing sugar over the tops of the tarts.

▨ COOK'S TIP

Always keep an eye on the 'best before' date of ground almonds; they lose their fragrant moistness quite quickly.

▨ COOK'S TIP

These rich tea-time treats are reputed to have been favourites with Queen Victoria and her household.

139 CUSTARD TARTS

Preparation time:
20 minutes

Cooking time:
28-35 minutes

Oven temperature:
200C/400F/gas 6
then 170C/325F/gas 3

Makes 8

Calories:
354 per portion

YOU WILL NEED:
6 oz Rich shortcrust pastry
  (see Introduction)
450 ml/¾ pint milk
2 eggs
2-3 teaspoons sugar
¼ teaspoon vanilla essence
grated nutmeg, to finish

Grease 8 patty tins. Roll out the pastry thinly and line the patty tins as for Balmoral tarts (recipe 138). Bake blind in a preheated oven for 12-15 minutes until set but not brown, then remove from the oven. Lower the heat to moderate.

Warm the milk over a low heat and meanwhile beat the eggs and sugar together. Stir the warm milk into the beaten eggs and flavour with vanilla. Strain the custard into the partially baked cases. Sprinkle the tops with grated nutmeg and return the tarts to the centre of the oven for 15-20 minutes until the custard is set. Serve cold.

140 CARLETON CAKES

Preparation time:
25 minutes

Cooking time:
about 15 minutes

Oven temperature:
200C/400F/gas 6

Makes 12

Calories:
147 per portion

YOU WILL NEED:
100 g/4 oz plain flour
25 g/1 oz ground rice
1 teaspoon baking powder
75 g/3 oz butter or margarine
50 g/2 oz caster sugar
2 eggs, separated
50 g/2 oz candied citron peel,
  chopped
25 g/1 oz blanched flaked
  almonds, shredded
3 tablespoons water
1 thin slice candied citron peel,
  to decorate

Sift the flour, rice and baking powder together. Cream the fat with the sugar until light and fluffy. Stir in the egg yolks and beat well. Mix in the flour, then the citron peel and almonds. Stir in the water and beat until smooth. Beat the egg whites until stiff but not brittle. Fold them into the mixture.

Spoon into well greased patty tins. Cut the citron peel slice into small wedges and place one in the centre of each cake. Bake in a preheated moderately hot oven for about 15 minutes. Remove from the tins and cool on a wire tray. Best when freshly baked.

■ COOK'S TIP

For these tarts small deep patty tins (about 5 cm/2 inches x 1.5 cm/½ inch) are preferable to the larger, shallower type.

■ COOK'S TIP

Citron is a kind of Mediterranean lemon with a very thick, rough skin, ideal for preserving or candying.

141 LEMON CURD AND CARAWAY CAKES

Preparation time:
20 minutes

Cooking time:
20 minutes

Oven temperature:
180C/350F/gas 4

Makes 30

Calories:
107 per portion

YOU WILL NEED:
150 g/6 oz soft margarine
100 g/4 oz caster sugar
150 g/6 oz lemon curd
225 g/8 oz self-raising flour
pinch of salt
1 teaspoon caraway seeds
3 eggs, beaten

Cream the margarine and sugar together until light and fluffy. Beat in the lemon curd. Sift the flour and salt and mix in the caraway seeds. Beat the eggs into the creamed mixture one at a time, with 2 tablespoons flour each time. Fold in the remaining flour.

Spoon the mixture into greased patty tins until three-quarters full. Bake in a preheated moderate oven for 20 minutes until golden and firm to the touch. Allow the cakes to shrink slightly, then remove from the tins and cool on a wire tray.

142 WALNUT BROWNIES

Preparation time:
15 minutes

Cooking time:
35 minutes

Oven temperature:
190C/375F/gas 5

Makes 16 squares

Calories:
164 per portion

YOU WILL NEED:
50 g/2 oz plain chocolate
75 g/3 oz butter
225 g/8 oz caster sugar
2 eggs, beaten
1 teaspoon vanilla essence
75 g/3 oz plain flour
½ teaspoon baking powder
½ teaspoon salt
50 g/2 oz walnuts, chopped

Grease and bottom-line a 20 cm/8 inch square tin.

Break up the chocolate and place in a mixing bowl with the butter and sugar. Place the bowl over a pan of hot water until the chocolate has melted.

Add the remaining ingredients and beat until smooth. Pour the mixture into the prepared tin.

Bake in a preheated oven for 35 minutes, until firm around the edges. Cool in the tin, then cut into squares. Eat the same day if possible.

■ COOK'S TIP

For *parties top with Lemon curd glacé icing: mix 75 g/3 oz sifted icing sugar with 3 teaspoons lemon curd into a spreading consistency. Swirl over the tops of the cakes and decorate with mimosa balls or a tiny crystallized lemon slice.*

■ COOK'S TIP

Other nuts which may be used instead of walnuts include pecans and hazelnuts.

143 FROSTED ORANGE SQUARES

Preparation time:
10 minutes

Cooking time:
1 hour

Oven temperature:
180C/350F/gas 4

Makes 20

Calories:
248 per portion

YOU WILL NEED:
225 g/8 oz butter, melted
300 ml/½ pint unsweetened
orange juice
275 g/10 oz caster sugar
2 eggs, beaten
400 g/14 oz self-raising flour
FOR THE TOPPING
100 g/4 oz icing sugar
3 tablespoons unsweetened orange
juice

Grease and bottom-line a 20 x 25 cm/8 x 10 inch roasting tin.

Place all the cake ingredients in a bowl. Beat well until smooth and evenly mixed.

Pour into the tin and bake in a preheated oven for 1 hour, until firm and golden brown.

To make the topping, place the icing sugar and orange juice in a bowl and beat together until smooth. Pour the topping over the warm cake and leave in the tin to cool completely.

When cold, cut into 5 cm/2 inch slices.

144 ROCK CAKES

Preparation time:
15 minutes

Cooking time:
12-15 minutes

Oven temperature:
230C/450F/gas 8

Makes 12

Calories:
182 per portion

YOU WILL NEED:
100 g/4 oz self-raising flour
100 g/4 oz wheatmeal flour
1 teaspoon baking powder
½ teaspoon salt
½ teaspoon grated nutmeg
100 g/4 oz butter or margarine
75 g/3 oz caster sugar
50 g/2 oz sultanas
1 egg, beaten
1-2 tablespoons milk

Place the flours, baking powder, salt and nutmeg in a bowl. Add the butter or margarine, cut into pieces, and rub into the flour until the mixture resembles fine breadcrumbs.

Stir in the sugar and sultanas. Add the beaten egg and mix until stiff, adding the milk if necessary.

Using 2 forks, place portions of the mixture in 12 rough heaps on a greased baking sheet.

Bake in a preheated oven for 12-15 minutes, until rich golden brown. Remove from the baking sheet and cool on a wire tray.

COOK'S TIP

Replace the butter with
250 ml/8 fl oz vegetable oil,
if liked.

COOK'S TIP

To enhance the 'fruity'
flavour of the rock cakes,
replace the nutmeg with the
finely grated zest of a
lemon.

145 MARBLED BARS

Preparation time:	YOU WILL NEED:
30 minutes	175 g/6 oz butter or margarine
	175 g/6 oz caster sugar
Cooking time:	3 eggs, beaten
25-30 minutes	175 g/6 oz self-raising flour
	few drops of red food colouring
Oven temperature:	1 tablespoon cocoa
180C/350F/gas 4	2 tablespoons boiling water
	FOR THE FUDGE ICING
Makes 24 bars	50 g/2 oz plain chocolate, broken up
	50 g/2 oz butter
Calories:	225 g/8 oz icing sugar, sifted
187 per portion	2 tablespoons milk

Grease an 18 x 28 cm/7 x 11 inch shallow oblong tin.

Place the butter or margarine and sugar in a bowl. Beat until light and fluffy. Beat in the eggs, a little at time. Add the flour to the mixture, folding in lightly using a metal spoon.

Divide the mixture in half. Colour one half pink with a few drops of red food colouring. Blend the cocoa with the water to a smooth paste and mix into the other half of the mixture.

Place alternate spoonfuls of each flavour side by side in the prepared tin. Swirl the two mixtures together with a skewer, then level off the top with a spoon. Bake in a preheated oven for 25-30 minutes, until risen and golden. Let cool in the tin.

Place all the fudge icing ingredients in a bowl over a pan of hot water. Stir until smooth and glossy, remove from the heat, and leave until thick enough for spreading. Spread evenly over the top of the cake, swirling it with a round-ended knife. Cut the cake into 3 down the length and 8 across to make 24 bars.

◼ COOK'S TIP

Omit the food colouring if you want a creamy colour to contrast with the chocolate.

146 NUTTY ANGELICA FANCIES

Preparation time:	YOU WILL NEED:
15-20 minutes	100 g/4 oz butter or margarine
	100 g/4 oz caster sugar
Cooking time:	2 eggs, lightly beaten
25-30 minutes	100 g/4 oz self-raising flour
	100 g/4 oz walnuts, chopped
Oven temperature:	75 g/3 oz angelica, chopped
180C/350F/gas 4	FOR THE ICING AND
	DECORATION
Makes 12	225 g/8 oz icing sugar, sifted
	2 tablespoons water
Calories:	25 g/1 oz walnuts, chopped
332 per portion	50 g/2 oz angelica, chopped

Cream the butter with the sugar until light and fluffy. Gradually beat in the eggs and fold in the flour, using a metal spoon. Mix together the walnuts and angelica and fold into the cake mixture. Divide the mixture between 12 greased dariole moulds.

Bake for 25-30 minutes in a preheated oven then turn out to cool on a wire rack.

To make the icing, mix the icing sugar with the water until thick and smooth. Drizzle over the top of each cake and sprinkle with a mixture of the chopped walnuts and angelica.

◼ COOK'S TIP

Place the filled dariole moulds on a baking tray for cooking to ease the lifting in and out of the oven.

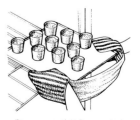

147 STRAWBERRY MILLE FEUILLES

Preparation time:
25 minutes

Cooking time:
20 minutes

Oven temperature:
220C/425F/gas 7

Makes 4-6

Calories:
922-615 per portion

YOU WILL NEED:
1 x 368 g/13 oz packet frozen puff
  pastry, defrosted
4 tablespoons strawberry jam
1 tablespoon Kirsch or orange juice
300 ml/½ pint double cream
2 teaspoons caster sugar
450 g/1 lb strawberries, halved
75 g/3 oz icing sugar

Roll out the pastry on a floured surface to a 20 x 25 cm/8 x 10 inch rectangle. Cut lengthways into three equal rectangles and place on dampened baking trays. Bake for 20 minutes until risen and golden. Cool on a wire rack.

Trim the rectangles to the same size, crushing any trimmings to use later. Mix the jam with the Kirsch or orange juice and whip the cream with the caster sugar.

Place one pastry strip on a serving plate. Top with half the jam, half the cream and one-third of the strawberries. Cover with a second pastry strip and repeat the filling. Finish with the third pastry strip.

Mix the icing sugar with a little water to make a paste and spread over the top. Sprinkle with a border of the crushed trimmings. Decorate with the remaining strawberries.

148 GREEK BAKLAVAS

Preparation time:
25 minutes

Cooking time:
25 minutes

Oven temperature:
200C/400F/gas 6

Makes 8

Calories:
435 per portion

YOU WILL NEED:
75 g/3 oz blanched almonds, finely
  chopped
75 g/3 oz walnuts finely chopped
½ teaspoon ground cinnamon
½ teaspoon ground mixed spice
150 ml/¼ pint clear honey
1 x 368 g/13 oz packet frozen puff
  pastry, defrosted
20 g/3/4 oz butter, melted
juice of ½ lemon

Mix the almonds with the walnuts, cinnamon, spice and 50 ml/2 fl oz of the honey. Roll out the pastry into a 33 cm/13 inch square. Cut into four squares. Place one square in a 16.5 cm/6½ inch shallow, square cake tin lined with foil. Brush with a little butter. Cover with another square then spread over the nut filling. Cover with the third square, brush again with butter then cover with the remaining square. Brush with butter and cut through the top two layers to mark out four squares. Cut each in half again to make triangles. Bake for 25 minutes.

Meanwhile, mix the lemon juice with the remaining honey and make up to 150 ml/¼ pint with water. Bring to the boil and simmer for 2 minutes. Spoon over the hot baklava still in its tin and leave to soak for 2 hours before removing from the tin to serve.

COOK'S TIP

To live up to its name of 'thousand leaves', Mille feuilles should have seemingly endless layers of flaky or puff pastry. To ensure that the pastry does rise well and evenly, cut the pastry with a sharp knife in one swift movement - never drag the knife through the pastry.

COOK'S TIP

To serve the baklavas cut through the bottom two layers of pastry with a sharp knife to make eight triangular baklavas - their typical shape.

149 APPLE STRUDEL

Preparation time:	YOU WILL NEED:
25 minutes, plus	*FOR THE STRUDEL PASTRY*
20-25 minutes	*150 g/5 oz plain flour*
standing time	*pinch of salt*
	2 teaspoons oil
Cooking time:	*½ egg, beaten*
20-25 minutes	*about 100 ml/4 fl oz warm water*
	FOR THE FILLING
Oven temperature:	*450 g/1 lb cooking apples, peeled,*
200C/400F/gas 6	*cored and sliced*
	50 g/2 oz currants
Serves 6	*50 g/2 oz sultanas*
	1 teaspoon ground cinnamon
Calories:	*3 tablespoons breadcrumbs, toasted*
209 per portion	*25 g/1 oz butter, melted*
	icing sugar to dust

Mix the flour with the salt in a large bowl. Make a well in the centre, add the oil, egg and 2-3 tablespoons of the water. Start to mix, adding more warm water to make a soft paste. Beat, using your hand, until smooth. Cover and leave for 15 minutes, then knead until very smooth.

Mix the apples with the currants, sultanas, cinnamon and 1 tablespoon of the breadcrumbs. Roll out the pastry on a floured surface to 1 cm/½ inch thickness. Lift on to a floured teacloth, leave for 8 minutes. Carefully stretch it until very thin. Brush with the butter and sprinkle with the crumbs. Scatter over the fruit and roll up. Place on a greased baking tray in a horseshoe shape and brush with butter. Bake for 20-25 minutes until golden. Dust with icing sugar and slice to serve.

150 LINZERTORTE

Preparation time:	YOU WILL NEED:
25 minutes	*150 g/6 oz plain flour*
	½ teaspoon ground cinnamon
Cooking time:	*75 g/3 oz butter*
25-30 minutes	*50 g/2 oz sugar*
	50 g/2 oz ground almonds
Oven temperature:	*2 teaspoons finely grated lemon rind*
190C/375F/gas 5	*2 large egg yolks*
	about 1 tablespoon lemon juice
Makes 1 x 18-20	*300 g/12 oz raspberry jam*
cm/7-8 inch tart	
Total calories:	
2468	

Sift the flour and cinnamon into a bowl. Rub in the butter until the mixture resembles fine breadcrumbs. Add the sugar, almonds and lemon rind. Bind the pastry with the egg yolks and enough lemon juice to make a stiff dough. Turn the dough on to a floured surface and knead lightly.

Roll two-thirds of the dough out and use to line an 18-20 cm/7-8 inch fluted flan ring on a baking tray. Make sure the dough is evenly rolled out, press to the shape of the ring and trim off the excess pastry. Fill the flan with the raspberry jam. Roll out the reserved pastry and trimmings and cut into strips with a pastry wheel or knife. Use these to make a lattice over the jam.

Bake in a moderately hot oven for 25-30 minutes until golden brown. Allow to cool, then remove the flan ring.

■ COOK'S TIP

Strudel pastry is a wafer-thin pastry. Use the fists of the hands to stretch the dough if you have long fingernails that are likely to puncture the dough.

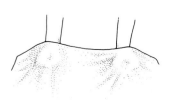

■ COOK'S TIP

Lattice pastry cutters are available to make pastry lattice easy: simply roll out the pastry and run the lattice cutter over it.

151 GOLDEN TREACLE TART

Preparation time:
20 minutes

Cooking time:
40 minutes

Oven temperature:
180C/350F/gas 4

Serves 4-6

Calories:
1046-697 per portion

YOU WILL NEED:
⅔ recipe Rich shortcrust pastry
(see Introduction)
450 g/1 lb golden syrup
2 teaspoons finely grated lemon rind
25 g/1 oz butter
4 tablespoons single cream
2 eggs, beaten
whipped cream, to decorate or
serve

Roll out the pastry on a floured surface and use to line a 20 cm/8 inch flan ring set on a baking tray.

Gently heat the syrup with the lemon rind until hand hot. Chop the butter and add to the mixture and stir to melt. Leave until almost cold.

Beat the cream and eggs together and fold into the cooled syrup. Mix well and pour into the flan case.

Bake for 40 minutes or until the pastry is crisp and the filling is set. Serve hot or cold with whipped cream.

◼ COOK'S TIP

To line a flan ring lift the pastry on to a rolling pin then lay it over the flan ring to gently unroll. Ease the pastry carefully into the sides, then roll the rolling

pin over the edge of the flan to cut off excess pastry. Pinch the pastry slightly at the top, raising it above the edge to allow for shrinkage during cooking.

152 CITRUS SPARKLE

Preparation time:
30 minutes, plus
standing and chilling
times

Cooking time:
20-25 minutes

Oven temperature:
220C/425F/gas 7

**Makes 1 x 23 cm/9
inch gâteau**

Total calories:
3866

YOU WILL NEED:
FOR THE ORANGE PASTRY:
225 g/8 oz plain flour
pinch of salt
finely grated rind and juice of
1 orange
175 g/6 oz butter, chilled and
grated
1 tablespoon iced water
FOR THE FILLING
thinly pared rind and juice of
1 lemon
2 tablespoons brandy
75 g/3 oz caster sugar
300 ml/½ pint double cream,
whipped
3 tablespoons lemon curd
sugared lemon slices, to decorate

Sift the flour with the salt, add the orange rind and butter and mix. Stir in the orange juice and water, knead lightly and chill for 30 minutes.

Meanwhile, mix the lemon rind, juice and brandy and leave to stand for 1 hour. Divide the pastry in half and roll each piece into a 23 cm/9 inch round. Prick then place on baking trays. Bake for 20-25 minutes until golden brown. Cool on the tray.

Strain the lemon mixture, add the sugar and stir to dissolve. Whisk into the cream then use half to sandwich the pastry rounds together with the lemon curd. Spread the remainder on top and decorate with sugared lemon slices.

◼ COOK'S TIP

This gâteau can also be sandwiched together with 3 tablespoons marmalade instead of the orange curd, if liked.

153 GLACE FANCIES

Preparation time:
25 minutes

Cooking time:
about 20 minutes

Oven temperature:
190C/375F/gas 5

Makes 44

Calories:
113 per portion

YOU WILL NEED:
*1 x recipe Victoria sandwich
    mixture (recipe 93)*
450 g/1 lb apricot jam
1 tablespoon water
FOR THE GLACE ICING
450 g/1 lb icing sugar, sifted
lemon juice, to mix
decorations (see Cook's Tip)

Grease and line a 30 x 20 cm/12 x 8 inch Swiss roll tin and pour in the Victoria sandwich mixture. Bake for about 20 minutes until golden and springy to touch. Let cool slightly then turn on to a wire tray. Peel off the paper and leave until cold. Trim the edges and cut the cake lengthways into 4 strips. Cut the first strip into 6 squares. Cut the second strip into 8 squares, then each square into 2 triangles. Cut the third strip into 8 squares and each square in half (2 rectangles). Cut the last strip into 6 rounds with a 4 cm/1½ inch pastry cutter.

Crumble the trimmings. Warm the jam with the water. Use a little to bind the crumbs together, then mould into marble-sized balls. Brush the remaining jam thinly over the sides of the cakes. Press a ball in the centre of some.

Make the glacé icing (see Introduction) and divide it into three bowls. Colour each bowlful as you wish. Put the cakes on a wire rack over a largish dish and pour over the icings.

■ COOK'S TIP

Decorate the cakes to suit your taste. Try crystallized flowers, angelica leaves, silver balls, glacé cherries, nuts, etc. Put the finished cakes into paper cases.

154 AURORA TARTLETS

Preparation time:
20 minutes, plus cooling

Cooking time:
15 minutes

Oven temperature:
200C/400F/gas 6

Makes 12

Calories:
287 per tart

YOU WILL NEED:
*1 x recipe Rich shortcrust pastry
    (see Introduction)*
*12 tablespoons Crème patissière
    (see Introduction)*
*12 canned peach halves
    redcurrant glaze (see Cook's Tip)*

Roll out the chilled pastry thinly and line 12 greased tartlet tins. Place on a baking sheet, prick well and line each one with a small piece of kitchen foil. Bake in a preheated oven for 10 minutes. Remove the foil and return the pastry to the oven for a further 5 minutes until crisp and golden. Lift out of the tartlet tins and cool on a wire rack.

Put a spoonful of crème patissière in each tartlet and place a peach half on top. Warm the redcurrant glaze and spoon or brush evenly over the peaches. Serve cold.

■ COOK'S TIP

For redcurrant glaze, melt 100 g/4 oz redcurrant jelly gently with 1 tablespoon lemon juice and 2 tablespoons water, or syrup from canned fruit. When the jam has melted, bring to the boil and boil until it drops off the edge of a wooden spoon in flakes.

155 MINCE PIES

Preparation time:
20 minutes

Cooking time:
12-15 minutes

Oven temperature:
220C/425F/gas 7

Makes 12

Calories:
241 per portion

YOU WILL NEED:
*1 x recipe Rich shortcrust pastry
  (see Introduction)
225 g/8 oz mincemeat
icing sugar, for dusting*

Roll out the pastry thinly (about 2.5 mm/⅛ inch thick). Cut out 12 rounds with a plain or fluted cutter and use to line 12 tartlet tins. Prick the bottom of each pie and put a spoonful of mincemeat in each one. Damp the edges. Cut out 12 more rounds with a size smaller cutter and use to cover the filling in each pie. Press down with the blunt edge of the smaller cutter so the lids are secure. Cut a small cross in the centre of each lid to allow the steam to escape.

Place the tartlet tins on a baking sheet and bake in a preheated oven for 12-15 minutes, until well risen and golden. Dust generously with icing sugar and serve hot. When cold, the mince pies can be stored in an airtight tin or frozen.

156 APPLE CHEESE CAKES

Preparation time:
25 minutes, plus cooling

Cooking time:
about 40 minutes

Oven temperature:
200C/400F/gas 6

Makes 12-15

Calories:
120-96 per portion

YOU WILL NEED:
*225 g/8 oz apples
4-5 tablespoons water
thinly peeled rind of ½ lemon
2-3 cloves
1 x 2.5 cm/1 inch piece cinnamon
  stick
1-2 tablespoons sugar
25 g/1 oz butter
scant 25 g/1 oz cake or fresh
  breadcrumbs
2 egg yolks or 1 whole egg, beaten
100 g/4 oz Rich shortcrust pastry
  (see Introduction)
caster sugar, for sprinkling*

Wash the apples and cut into small chunks, removing the stem and core, but leaving the peel. Cover the base of the pan with water, add the apples, lemon rind, cloves, cinnamon and sugar. Cover and cook until softened. Remove the lid and continue cooking into a thick pulp, stirring frequently so it does not stick. Remove the cinnamon stick.

Sieve the pulp and return the pan over gentle heat. Add the butter and, when melted, remove the pan from the heat. Cool slightly then stir in the crumbs and egg. Leave until cold.

Roll out the pastry thinly and line 12-15 tartlet tins. Prick the bottoms and three-quarters fill with the apple mixture. Bake in a preheated oven for 15 minutes, or until the pastry is crisp and the filling set. Remove from the tins and cool on a wire tray. When cold, sprinkle generously with caster sugar.

■ COOK'S TIP

If using bought mincemeat, add a dash of rum or brandy to it, or, if you prefer something non-alcoholic, a little lemon juice.

■ COOK'S TIP

Cooking fruit into a thick, well-flavoured purée called 'cheese' was a preserving method often used in the days before the freezer. If you do not have stick cinnamon, use a pinch of ground cinnamon in this recipe.

BIG OCCASION CAKES

Special occasions need special cakes. This chapter includes cakes and gâteaux, rich in creams, fruits, nuts, liqueurs and spices, ideal for any celebration teatime.

157 ALADDIN'S CAVE GATEAU

Preparation time: 30 minutes	YOU WILL NEED: 4 eggs 100 g/4 oz caster sugar
Cooking time: 15 minutes	100 g/4 oz self-raising flour ¼ teaspoon salt FOR THE FILLING
Oven temperature: 190C/375F/gas 5	300 ml/½ pint double cream, whipped
Makes 1 rectangular gâteau	2 teaspoons caster sugar 350 g/12 oz prepared soft fruits 25 g/1 oz icing sugar, sifted a few fruits with stems for
Total calories: 2631	decoration (optional)

Place the eggs and sugar in a bowl set over a pan of hot water and whisk until thick. Sift the flour with the salt. Remove the bowl from the heat and fold in the flour. Pour into a greased and floured 35 x 20 cm/14 x 8 inch rectangular cake tin and bake for 15 minutes. Cool on a wire rack.

Carefully cut the sponge vertically in half and spread the bottom layer with whipped cream. Sprinkle with the caster sugar. Carefully position the second sponge layer on top of the cream at an angle so that its edge rests on the side of the plate and looks like an open jewellery box. Fill the open sponge and cream centre with the prepared fruit, allowing it to spill over the edge of the cake. Chill lightly before serving.

158 VALENTINE CAKE

Preparation time: about 45 minutes	YOU WILL NEED: 2 recipes plain or pink Victoria Sandwich mixture (see recipe 93)
Cooking time: 1½-1¾ hours	100 g/4 oz strawberry jam 1 x 23 cm/9 inch heart-shaped cake board
Oven temperature: 180C/350F/gas 4	1 recipe Apricot glaze (see Introduction) ⅔ recipe pink Satin icing
Makes 1 x 20 cm/ 8 inch heart-shaped cake	(see Introduction) 100 g/4 oz Royal icing (see Introduction)
Total calories: 7326	3 pink moulded roses,or crystallized rose petals, to decorate

Turn the prepared cake mixture into a greased and lined 20 cm/8 inch heart-shaped tin. Bake for 1½-1¾ hours. Cool on a wire rack.

Cut the cake in half horizontally and sandwich together with the jam. Place on the cake board and brush the top and the sides with the apricot glaze.

Roll out the satin icing on a surface dusted with icing sugar until thin then press on to the cake to cover. Cut off any surplus icing.

Put the royal icing in a piping bag fitted with a No. 2 writing nozzle and pipe a line 1 cm/½ inch in from the edge of the cake. Pipe dots each side of the line. Decorate with roses.

■ COOK'S TIP

Hulled raspberries, strawberries and blackberries along with topped and tailed red and blackcurrants make the ideal filling for this cake.

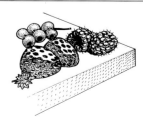

■ COOK'S TIP

For a smooth professional finish to the icing, dip your hands in icing sugar and press the icing on to the cake, rubbing with a circular motion.

159 RICH CELEBRATION CAKE

Preparation time:	YOU WILL NEED:
25 minutes	275 g/10 oz butter
	275 g/10 oz soft brown sugar
Cooking time:	grated rind of ½ lemon
3½ hours	5 large eggs, beaten
	350 g/12 oz plain flour
Oven temperature:	½ teaspoon ground mixed spice
150C/300F/gas 2	½ teaspoon ground cinnamon
	450 g/1 lb currants
Makes 1 x 20 cm/	200 g/7 oz sultanas
8 inch round or 1 x	200 g/7 oz raisins
18 cm/7 inch square	150 g/5 oz glacé cherries, halved
cake	75 g/3 oz chopped mixed peel
	75 g/3 oz flaked almonds
Total calories:	2 tablespoons brandy
7732	

Cream the butter with the sugar until light and fluffy. Beat in the lemon rind and eggs with a little of the flour. Sift the remaining flour with the mixed spice and cinnamon and fold into the creamed mixture. Fold in the fruit, nuts and brandy, mixing well. Spoon into a greased and lined 20 cm/8 inch round or 18 cm/7 inch square cake tin.

Bake for 3½ hours or until a skewer inserted into the centre comes out clean. Allow to cool slightly in the tin, then transfer to a wire rack to cool completely.

Decorate as liked. For a traditional almond paste and royal icing decoration you will need 550 g/1¼ lb Almond paste and 675 g/1½ lb Royal icing (see Introduction).

160 RICH CHOCOLATE GATEAU

Preparation time:	YOU WILL NEED:
30 minutes	1 x 23 cm/9 inch chocolate
	Whisked sponge cake
Cooking time:	(see Introduction)
35-40 minutes	FOR THE CHOCOLATE
	MERINGUE BUTTER ICING
Oven temperature:	2 egg whites
190C/375F/gas 5	100 g/4 oz icing sugar, sifted
	100 g/4 oz unsalted butter
Makes 1 x 23 cm/	50 g/2 oz plain chocolate, melted
9 inch gâteau	75 g/3 oz chocolate caraque
	(see Cook's Tip)
Total calories:	
2088	

Sift the cooked sponge cake in half. To make the meringue butter icing, place the egg whites and icing sugar in a bowl over a saucepan of simmering water and whisk until the mixture holds its shape. Cool slightly. Cream the butter until soft and light then beat into the meringue mixture with the melted chocolate.

Sandwich the cakes together with some of the meringue butter icing and use the rest to cover the cake. Decorate with the chocolate caraque.

COOK'S TIP

When spooning the mixture into the cake tin, make a slight hollow in the centre of the mixture to enable the cake to rise evenly.

COOK'S TIP

To make chocolate caraque, pour a thin layer of chocolate on to a marble slab or cold surface and cool until it begins to set and go cloudy. Using a sharp, thin-bladed knife at a slight angle, push it across the chocolate with a slight sawing movement, scraping off a thin layer to form a long scroll.

161 DARK GINGER CAKE

Preparation time:
45 minutes, plus
standing

Cooking time:
about 1¼ hours

Oven temperature:
160C/325F/gas 3

**Makes 1 x 23 x 13
cm/9 x 5 inch cake**

Total calories:
3796

YOU WILL NEED:
175 g/6 oz black treacle
40 g/1½ oz demerara sugar
75 g/3 oz butter or hard margarine
175 g/6 oz plain flour
2 teaspoons ground ginger
1 teaspoon mixed spice
½ teaspoon bicarbonate of soda
2 eggs
100 ml/4 fl oz milk or buttermilk
ginger crème au beurre
  (see Cook's Tip)
a few pieces of stem or
  crystallized ginger

Grease and line a 23 x 13 cm/9 x 5 inch loaf tin.

Put the treacle, sugar and butter or margarine into a pan and heat gently until melted then allow to cool slightly. Sift the flour, ginger, spice and bicarbonate of soda into a bowl and make a well in the centre. Add the eggs and milk or buttermilk and the melted treacle mixture and beat until smooth. Pour into the tin, and bake in a preheated oven for about 1¼ hours or until a skewer inserted in the centre comes out clean.

Turn out on to a wire tray and leave until cold; then wrap in foil and store for at least 24 hours before decorating and eating.

Make the crème au beurre and spread or pipe over the top of the cake. Decorate with pieces of ginger.

■ COOK'S TIP

For ginger crème au beurre,
make the crème au beurre
given in recipe 82, replacing
the vanilla essence with a
pinch of ground ginger.

162 CHOCOLATE CHESTNUT LAYER

Preparation time:
45 minutes

Cooking time:
20-25 minutes

Oven temperature:
190C/375F/gas 5

**Makes 1 x 20 cm/
8 inch long gâteau**

Total calories:
2553

YOU WILL NEED:
1 recipe chocolate Whisked
  sponge mixture (see Introduction)
1 x 227 g/8 oz can unsweetened
  chestnut purée
1 tablespoon clear honey
175 ml/6 fl oz double cream
2 tablespoons Cointreau
100 g/4 oz chocolate curls
chocolate leaves

Turn the whisked sponge mixture into a greased and lined 20 x 30 cm/8 x 12 inch Swiss roll tin and bake for 20-25 minutes. Cool on a wire rack. Place the chestnut purée, honey and 2 tablespoons of the cream in a bowl and whip thoroughly. Whip the remaining cream until stiff then whisk in half the purée mixture and Cointreau.

Cut the cake into three 20 cm/8 inch long pieces and sandwich together with one third of the cream mixture. Cover the sides with more cream and coat with chocolate curls. Spread the remaining cream mixture over the top of the cake and draw lines across with a palette knife. Pipe the remaining chestnut purée mixture around the edge of the cake and decorate with chocolate leaves.

■ COOK'S TIP

To make chocolate curls for   *the curls will not form*
the sides of this cake, use a   *properly and will break.*
potato peeler to scrape curls
directly from a block of
chocolate. Make sure the
chocolate is not too cold or

163 CARRIBEAN RUM SANDWICH

Preparation time:
about 30 minutes

Cooking time:
about 15 minutes

Oven temperature:
190C/375F/gas 5

Makes 1 x 20 cm/8 inch round cake

Total calories:
3666

YOU WILL NEED:
175 g/6 oz caster sugar
175 g/6 oz soft margarine
3 eggs
175 g/6 oz self-raising flour
1½ teaspoons baking powder
1 tablespoon rum
FOR THE FILLING
1 x 375 g/13 oz can crushed
    pineapple
1½ teaspoons arrowroot
150 ml/¼ pint double cream
1-2 tablespoons rum

Grease and base line three 20 cm/8 inch round sandwich tins.

Put the sugar, margarine and eggs into a bowl and sift in the flour and baking powder. Add the rum. Beat until quite smooth. Divide the mixture between the tins and level the tops. Bake in a preheated oven for about 15 minutes or until well risen and firm to the touch. Turn out on to a wire tray and leave until cold. Strip off the paper.

For the filling, blend 1-2 tablespoons pineapple juice with the arrowroot. Heat the rest of the contents of the can to just below boiling. Add the arrowroot and bring to the boil, stirring till thickened and clear. Whip the cream and rum together and then fold half through the cooled pineapple mixture with half the almonds. Spread the pineapple mixture over two layers of cake and place one on top of the other. Top with the remaining layer and spread the remaining cream over.

■ COOK'S TIP

To decorate this cake, sprinkle toasted almond flakes over the top and add a few pieces of glacé pineapple, if available.

164 APRICOT CAROB CAKE

Preparation time:
40 minutes

Cooking time:
15-20 minutes

Oven temperature:
190C/375F/gas 5

Makes 1 x 20 cm/8 inch round cake

Total calories: 5829

YOU WILL NEED:
175 g/6 oz butter or hard margarine
175 g/6 oz caster sugar
150 g/5 oz self-raising flour
1 teaspoon baking powder
25 g/1 oz carob powder
3 eggs
1 tablespoon water
about 350 g/12 oz apricot jam
spiced Butter icing
    (see Cook's Tip)
icing sugar, for dredgingsifted
¼-½ teaspoon mixed spice

Grease and base line three 20 cm/8 inch round sandwich tins.

Cream the fat and sugar until light, fluffy and pale. Sift the flour, baking powder and carob powder together. Beat the eggs into the creamed mixture, one at a time, following each with a spoonful of flour. Fold in the remaining flour, then the water.

Divide the mixture between the tins, level the tops, and bake in a preheated oven for 15-20 minutes or until well risen and just firm to the touch. Turn out on to a wire tray to cool.

Make up the spiced Butter icing. Spread a layer of jam and butter cream over 2 of the cakes and sandwich together.

Using a 2.5 cm/1 inch plain round cutter, cut out 6 circles about 2 cm/¾ inch in from the edge of the remaining cake. Place on the top and dredge with icing sugar. Pipe a whirl of the remaining butter icing in each hole. Dredge the remaining small circles of cake with icing sugar and place on top of the piped cream. Pipe the last butter icing between the circles.

■ COOK'S TIP

Make up 1 quantity of Butter icing (see Introduction), adding a scant ½ teaspoon mixed spice with the icing sugar.

165 GRANNY CAKE

Preparation time:	YOU WILL NEED:
about 45 minutes,	175 g/6 oz butter or margarine
plus drying	175 g/6 oz caster sugar
overnight	grated rind of 2 oranges
	3 eggs
Cooking time:	250 g/9 oz self-raising flour
1-1¼ hours	1½ teaspoons baking powder
	FOR THE FILLING AND ICING
Oven temperature:	50 g/2 oz butter
180C/350F/gas 4	75 g/3 oz icing sugar, sifted
	grated rind of 1 large orange
Makes 1 x 20 cm/8	100 g/4 oz ground almonds
inch round cake	4 tablespoons orange juice
	225 g/8 oz almond paste
Total calories:	red and yellow food colouring
6340	⅔ recipe Fondant icing
	(see recipe 169)
	2-3 tablespoons apricot jam
	moulded leaves and flowers

Place all the cake ingredients in a bowl and beat until smooth. Turn into a greased and base-lined 20 cm/8 inch round cake tin and bake for 1-1¼ hours. Cool.

Cream the butter with the icing sugar, orange rind, almonds and juice until fluffy. Halve the cake and sandwich together again with this filling. Cover the cake with the almond paste and dry overnight.

Colour and roll out the fondant icing, brush the cake with the jam and then cover the cake with the icing. Leave to dry then decorate with moulded leaves and flowers and ribbon.

▍ COOK'S TIP

For moulded flowers, press small pieces of fondant icing between fingers dipped in cornflour. Shape into petals. Roll one petal to form a flower centre.

Mould more petals around the centre. Cut off the base if the petals become too thick. Allow to harden. Highlight the centre with food colouring.

166 SILVER WEDDING CAKE

Preparation time:	YOU WILL NEED:
Make 2-3 months in	1 x 23 cm/9 inch square Basic fruit
advance	cake (see Introduction)
	FOR THE ICING AND
Cooking time:	DECORATION
3-5 hours	1 recipe Almond paste
	(see Introduction)
Oven temperature:	1 x 25 cm/10 inch square silver
140C/275F/gas 1	cake board
	1 recipe Royal icing
Makes 1 x 23 cm/9	(see Introduction)
inch square cake	crystallized flowers
	silver cake decorations
Total calories:	silver cake board edging
15128	

Make the cake as directed and leave to mature for 2-3 months.

Cover the cake with the almond paste 1-2 weeks before icing and place on the silver cake board. Make up the icing and flat ice the cake. Decorate with crystallized flowers and silver cake decorations as in the photograph. Place the silver cake board edging around the sides of the cake, securing with a little icing. Pipe a shell border on the top and bottom edges of the cake to finish.

▍ COOK'S TIP

To secure the cake board edging, using a small palette knife, spread a thin layer of icing around the edge of the board. Before it dries, press on the edging.

167 CHRISTENING CAKE

Preparation time:
Make 2-3 months in advance

Cooking time:
3½ hours

Oven temperature:
150C/300F/gas 2

Makes 1 x 20 cm/8 inch cake

Total calories:
11824

YOU WILL NEED:
1 x 20 cm/8 inch round Rich celebration cake (see recipe 159)
FOR THE ICING AND DECORATION
550 g/1¼ lb Almond paste (see Introduction)
1 x 23 cm/9 inch round silver cake board
675 g/1½ lb Royal icing (see Introduction)
pink food colouring

Make the cake as directed, bake and leave to mature for 2-3 months. Cover with the almond paste, 1-2 weeks before icing.

Reserve a little of the icing for piping and colour the remainder pink. Flat ice the cake with the pink icing. Cover the silver board with a thin layer of icing and leave to dry hard. Position the cake on top.

Cut a strip of greaseproof paper the circumference and depth of the sides of the cake and draw a scalloped edge evenly all the way round. Secure on to the cake with a pin and prick through the design on to the cake. Remove the paper and pipe dots of the white icing on to the cake following the scalloped design, piping a few vertical dots between each scallop. Pipe a trellis along the bottom and a line of small dots either side. Write the child's name on top and finish with stars on the edge.

◼ COOK'S TIP

To pipe a trellis on the bottom edge of the cake, pipe a series of parallel lines at an angle all around the cake, then pipe another layer of parallel lines over the top in the opposite direction.

168 EIGHTEENTH BIRTHDAY CAKE

Preparation time:
Make 2-3 months in advance

Cooking time:
3½ hours

Oven temperature:
150C/300F/gas 2

Makes 1 x 20 cm/8 inch cake

Total calories: 12612

YOU WILL NEED:
1 x 20 cm/8 inch round Rich celebration cake (see recipe 159)
FOR THE ICING AND DECORATION
550 g/1¼lb Almond paste (see Introduction)
675 g/1½ lb Royal icing (see Introduction)
1 x 23 cm/9 inch round silver cake board
green food colouring
silver key

Make the cake as directed, bake and leave to mature for 2-3 months. Cover the cake with the almond paste, 1-2 weeks before icing. Make up the icing and reserve a little white icing for piping. Colour the remainder pale green. Flat ice the cake with the green icing as shown, using a serrated scraper on the sides of the cake to give a ridged effect. Using a palette knife, cover the board with a layer of icing. Place the cake on top.

Using a greaseproof paper bag fitted with a star-shaped nozzle, pipe a shell border with the white icing around the top and bottom edges of the cake. Then using a writing nozzle, pipe CONGRATULATIONS on top of the cake. Pipe three parallel lines beside the word. When these are dry pipe another line on top of each to give a bolder design. Add the silver key.

◼ COOK'S TIP

When writing with icing, have the royal icing on the soft side so it flows smoothly and freely . Hold the nozzle about 2.5 cm/1 inch from the cake.

169 FONDANT-ICED CHRISTMAS CAKE

Preparation time: Make 2-3 months in advance	YOU WILL NEED: *1 x 20 cm/8 inch round Rich celebration cake (see recipe 159)* FOR THE ICING AND DECORATION
Cooking time: 3½ hours	*550 g/1¼ lb Almond paste (see Introduction)*
Oven temperature: 150C/300F/gas 2	*1 x 23 cm/9 inch round silver cake board* *350 g/12 oz icing sugar, sifted*
Makes 1 x 20 cm/ 8 inch round cake	*1 egg white* *1 tablespoon liquid glucose, warmed* *icing sugar*
Total calories: 10948	*egg white, to brush cake* *red and green food colourings*

Bake the cake and leave to mature 2-3 months. Cover with Almond paste 1-2 weeks before icing and place on the board.

To make the fondant icing, place the icing sugar, egg white and glucose in a bowl and mix, using a palette knife, until a dough is formed. Knead lightly until smooth. Roll out on a surface dusted with icing sugar. Brush the cake with egg white and cover with the icing, reserving any trimmings. Allow to dry overnight.

Colour a little of the reserved trimmings with green and some red and mould to resemble holly. Arrange in a circle on top of the cake and secure a candle in the centre. Tie a ribbon around the cake to complete.

■ COOK'S TIP

It is essential to allow the icing to dry overnight before adding the coloured decorations or their colours will run into the white icing, giving a poor finish.

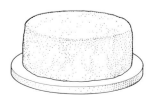

170 MOTHER'S DAY CAKE

Preparation time: 25 minutes	YOU WILL NEED: *175 g/6 oz butter or margarine* *175 g/6 oz caster sugar*
Cooking time: 1¼ hours	*3 eggs* *100 g/4 oz glacé cherries* *50 g/2 oz crystallized ginger, chopped*
Oven temperature: 160C/325F/gas 3	*50 g/2 oz crystallized pineapple, chopped* *50 g/2 oz citron peel, chopped*
Makes 1 x 20 cm/ 8 inch cake	*225 g/8 oz self-raising flour* FOR THE ICING AND DECORATION
Total calories: 3930	*225 g/8 oz icing sugar, sifted* *2-3 tablespoons water* *50 g/2 oz glacé cherries* *2 tablespoons caster sugar* *few pieces of angelica*

Cream the butter sugar until light and fluffy. Gradually beat in the eggs. Wash, drain and chop the cherries. Add to the other chopped ingredients and coat in 2 tablespoons of the flour. Sift the flour over the creamed mixture and fold in gently with a metal spoon. Gently fold in the chopped ingredients. Spoon into a greased and lined 20 cm/8 inch round cake tin. Bake for 1¼ hours then turn out to cool on a wire rack.

Mix the icing sugar with the water and spoon over the cake, allowing it to drizzle down the sides. Coat the glacé cherries in caster sugar and place small pieces of angelica on top of them to form stalks. Arrange the cherries decoratively on top of the cake.

■ COOK'S TIP

When time is short simply decorate the top of this cake with a few fresh spring flowers or pale coloured roses. Allow the icing to set first and place the flowers on top just before serving.

171 SIMNEL CAKE

Preparation time:	YOU WILL NEED:
Make 2-3 months in	*mixture for 20 cm/8 inch round*
advance	*Rich celebration cake*
	(see recipe 159)
Cooking time:	*550 g/1¼ lb Almond paste*
3½ hours	*(see Introduction)*
	2 tablespoons apricot jam, sieved
Oven temperature:	*beaten egg white, to glaze*
150C/300F/gas 2	*1 tablespoon caster sugar*
	FOR THE DECORATION
Makes 1 x 20 cm/	*100 g/4 oz icing sugar*
8 inch round cake	*1-2 tablespoons water*
	ribbon
Total calories:	
10087	

Make up the cake mixture and place half in a 20 cm/8 inch round cake tin. Roll out 275 g/10 oz of the almond paste and place on top of the cake mixture. Cover with the remaining mixture and bake in a preheated oven for 3½ hours. Let cool on a wire rack.

Brush the top of the cake with the jam. Roll out half of the remaining almond paste amd place on top of the cake. Crimp the edges decoratively. Shape the remaining almond paste into 11 balls and place around the top edge of the cake. Brush the almond paste with the egg white. Sprinkle with caster sugar, place under a hot grill and cook until light golden. Cool.

Mix the icing sugar with the water to make a thick icing and spread in the centre of the cake. Leave to set. Tie a ribbon around the cake to complete.

▨ COOK'S TIP

The significance of the balls on top of this Easter cake is that they represent Jesus Christ's eleven 'good' disciples. The 12th disiciple, Judas Iscariot, is left off.

172 CHOCOLATE PIGGY CAKE

Preparation time:	YOU WILL NEED:
40 minutes	*1 x 18 cm/7 inch baked Victoria*
	sandwich mixture (see recipe 93)
Cooking time:	FOR THE FILLING AND
20-25 minutes	DECORATION
	3 tablespoons raspberry jam
Oven temperature:	*1 recipe Butter icing*
180C/350F/gas 4	*(see Introduction)*
	pink or blue food colouring
Makes 1 x 18 cm/	*1 tablespoon cocoa powder*
7 inch round cake	*boiling water*
	225 g//8 oz almond paste
Total calories:	*icing sugar, for dusting*
4654	*candles*

Sandwich the cake layers together with the raspberry jam. Colour the butter icing a pale shade of either pink or blue. Mix the cocoa to a cream with a little boiling water. Knead the almond paste until pliable, then gradually knead in the cocoa cream. Roll out on to a surface dusted with icing sugar and, using a pig-shaped biscuit cutter, cut out eight pigs from the almond paste.

Cover the top and sides of the cake with some icing. Mark the top of the cake with a round-bladed knife and the sides with a serrated scraper. Using a greaseproof paper bag fitted with a star-shaped nozzle, pipe the edging on the cake as shown in the photograph. Arrange the chocolate pigs around the side of the cake and the candles on top.

▨ COOK'S TIP

You can, if liked, cut out different animals to place around the side of this cake - for example, circus animals, cats, dogs or mice! Cut out using special animal-shaped cutters or a free-hand design.

173 NUMERAL CAKE

Preparation time: about 1 hour	YOU WILL NEED: *1 recipe Victoria sandwich mixture (see recipe 93)*
Cooking time: 20-25 minutes	FOR THE ICING AND DECORATION *2 recipes Butter icing (see Introduction)*
Oven temperature: 180C/350F/gas 4	*food colouring coloured sweets or chocolate buttons*
Makes 1 numeral cake	*candles*

Total calories:
5076

Make up and bake the Victoria sandwich cake as directed. Cut out two 18 cm/7 inch rounds of greaseproof paper, overlap slightly at one end and pin together. Draw the shape of the figure 3 on the two pieces of paper and mark a dotted line at the point where they overlap. Use as much of the area as possible when drawing the numeral. Unpin the pieces of paper and cut out the shapes that have been drawn. Use these as a pattern to cut out the shape from the two sandwich cakes.

Fit the cake together on a board. Colour the butter icing as wished. Reserve a quarter of the butter icing for piping and use the remainder to cover the cake. Pipe stars or scrolls around the cake with the reserved icing, decorate with the sweets and appropriate number of candles.

▨ COOK'S TIP

Other numerals can be cut out from the cake. A figure 8 may be made simply by cutting out a 7.5 cm/3 inch round from the middle of each cake. The ends of the cake should be cut off slightly where they fit together. A figure 6 may be cut out of the cake which has already been sandwiched together.

174 KITTEN CAKE

Preparation time: 40 minutes	YOU WILL NEED: *2 recipes Victoria sandwich mixture (see recipe 93)*
Cooking time: 1¼-1½ hours	*1 recipe chocolate Butter icing (see Introduction)*
	3 sponge fingers
Oven temperature: 180C/350F/gas 4	*2 ice cream cones liquorice sweets liquorice ribbon*
Makes 1 kitten cake	*few short pieces spaghetti*

Total calories:
5612

Make up the cake mixture as directed and use to three-quarters fill a greased 600 ml/1 pint and 1.2 litre/2 pint pudding basin. Bake for 1 hour and 1¼-1½ hours respectively, Allow to cool.

Trim the small cake into a ball for the head. Trim a slice from one side of the large cake to flatten the chest. Place the large cake on a cake board or plate and fix the small one on top with a little butter icing. Position a sponge finger at the side for a tail.

Cut a 1 cm/½ inch slice off the other sponge fingers. Place the sponge fingers on either side of the chest as legs; position the slices as paws. Cut the tips off the ice cream cones and use for ears. Cover the kitten with the butter icing. Shape the sweets for the eyes and nose; press into position. Tie the liquorice ribbon around the kitten's neck and use the spaghetti as whiskers.

▨ COOK'S TIP

Although the kitten in this recipe has been covered with chocolate butter icing to represent brown fur, it is possible to make a white cat with plain butter icing or even a striped or multi-coloured cat using plain and chocolate butter icing if liked- the limit is your own imagination.

175 MALAKOFF GATEAU

Preparation time:	YOU WILL NEED:
about 30 minutes, plus chilling	1½-2 packets sponge finger biscuits
	150 g/5 oz blanched almonds, roughly chopped
Serves 8-10	100 g/4 oz caster sugar
	175 g/6 oz butter
Calories:	2 egg yolks
607-486 per portion	6 tablespoons brandy or dark rum
	5 tablespoons milk
	300 ml/½ pint whipping cream
	slivers of blanched almonds, toasted
	natural glacé cherries

Grease and line a 23 x 12.5 cm/9 x 5 inch loaf tin. Cover the base with sponge finger biscuits. Put the almonds and 50 g/2 oz of the sugar in a heavy-based pan and heat gently until the sugar turns a light caramel colour. Turn on to an oiled baking sheet, leave until cold and then crush finely with a rolling pin.

Cream the butter until soft then add the remaining sugar and beat until light and fluffy. Beat in the egg yolks alternating with 3 tablespoons brandy or rum; stir in the crushed nuts.

Combine the milk and remaining brandy or rum and sprinkle 2 tablespoons over the biscuits in the tin, then spread with half the nut mixture. Add a second layer of sponge finger biscuits, sprinkle with another 2 tablespoons milk mixture and cover with remaining nut mixture. Lay a final layer of biscuits on top and sprinkle with the remaining milk mixture. Press down evenly then cover with a sheet of greased greaseproof or non-stick silicone paper; then with foil. If possible, put a light weight on the mixture and chill for at least 12 hours.

▨ COOK'S TIP

To decorate the gâteau, turn it out on to a plate and carefully peel off the paper. Whip the cream and spread half of it over the gâteau. Use the remainder to pipe diagonal lines on top. Sprinkle toasted almonds between the lines and decorate with glacé cherries.

176 SACHERTORTE

Preparation time:	YOU WILL NEED:
50 minutes	100 g/4 oz butter
	175 g/6 oz caster sugar
Cooking time:	175 g/6 oz plain chocolate, melted
50-60 minutes	1 teaspoon vanilla essence
	6 egg yolks
Oven temperature:	75 g/3 oz plain flour
180C/350F/gas 4	8 egg whites
	6 tablespoons apricot jam, warmed
Makes 1 x 23 cm/	FOR THE CHOCOLATE ICING
9 inch gâteau	225 g/8 oz plain chocolate
	100 ml/4 fl oz double cream
Total calories:	350 g/12 oz icing sugar, sifted
6574	whipped cream and chocolate curls, to decorate

Cream the butter with the sugar until light and fluffy. Beat in the melted chocolate and vanilla. Gradually add the egg yolks and fold in the flour. Whisk the egg whites until stiff and fold in. Spoon into a greased and floured 23 cm/9 inch loose-bottomed cake tin and bake for 50-60 minutes. Leave to cool in the tin for 30 minutes then turn out on to a wire rack.

Slice the cake horizontally and sandwich together with the warmed apricot jam.

Melt the chocolate in a bowl over hot water, then beat in the cream and icing sugar. Allow to cool for 10 minutes then spread over the top and sides of the cake. Leave to set for 30 minutes then decorate with swirls of cream and chocolate curls.

▨ COOK'S TIP

A smooth finish to the icing can be achieved if a wet palette knife is smoothed across the surface after spreading.

177 AUSTRIAN COFFEE GATEAU

Preparation time:	YOU WILL NEED:
30 minutes	*100 g/4 oz butter or margarine*
	100 g/4 oz caster sugar
Cooking time:	*2 eggs*
40-50 minutes	*100 g/4 oz self-raising flour*
	2 tablespoons coffee essence
Oven temperature:	*grated rind of 1 lemon*
160C/325F/gas 3	*FOR THE SYRUP*
	150 ml/¼ pint black coffee
Makes 1 x 20 cm/	*50 g/2 oz caster sugar*
8 inch ring cake	*1 tablespoon brandy*
	FOR THE DECORATION
Total calories:	*300 ml/½ pint double cream*
3000	*chocolate curls (recipe 162)*

Cream the butter with the sugar until light and fluffy. Add the eggs, one at a time, adding a little flour with the second egg. Beat in the coffee essence, then fold in the remaining flour with the lemon rind. Turn into a greased 20 cm/8 inch ring tin and bake for 40-50 minutes. Turn out to cool on a wire rack.

To make the syrup, heat the coffee with the sugar until dissolved. Add the brandy and simmer for 5 minutes. Cool. Prick the cake with a skewer and pour over the syrup, a little at a time, until it is all absorbed.

Whip the cream and spread a little all over the cake. Pipe the remainder around the edge of the cake and decorate with chocolate curls.

■ COOK'S TIP

Place the cake on a wire rack with a large plate underneath to catch the syrup. This can be saved and poured over the cake again until all is absorbed.

178 DOUBLE CHOCOLATE DEVIL'S FOOD CAKE

Preparation time:	YOU WILL NEED:
20 minutes	*50 g/2 oz cocoa*
	6 tablespoons boiling water
Cooking time:	*175 g/6 oz self-raising flour*
30-35 minutes	*2 teaspoons baking powder*
	175 g/6 oz caster sugar
Oven temperature:	*175 g/6 oz soft margarine*
180C/350F/gas 4	*4 eggs*
	FOR THE FILLING AND ICING
Serves 8-10	*450 g/1 lb icing sugar, sifted*
	100 g/4 oz plain chocolate, broken
Calories:	*in pieces*
747-598 per portion	*50 g/2 oz butter*
	4 tablespoons milk

Grease and base-line two 20 cm/8 inch sandwich tins.

Blend the cocoa and boiling water to a smooth paste. Place in a bowl with the flour, baking powder, sugar, margarine and eggs. Beat until light and fluffy. Divide the mixture between the prepared tins and smooth the tops. Bake in a preheated oven for 30-35 minutes, until well risen and firm. Leave the cake in the tins 1 minute, then turn out on to a wire tray to cool.

For the filling and icing, stir the sugar, chocolate, butter and milk together in a bowl over a pan of hot water until melted to a smooth icing. Cool for 15 minutes, then beat well until thickened. Fill the cake with a little icing, then spread the remaining icing evenly over the top and sides.

■ COOK'S TIP

Use a palette knife to spread the icing over the cake and to make 'swirls' in the icing.

179 ROUND BATTENBURG CAKE

Preparation time:
25 minutes

Cooking time:
30-35 minutes

Oven temperature:
180C/350F/gas 4

Serves 8-10

Calories:
558-446 per portion

YOU WILL NEED:
175 g/6 oz self-raising flour
1 teaspoon baking powder
175 g/6 oz caster sugar
175 g/6 oz soft margarine
3 eggs
few drops of red food colouring
FOR THE FILLING AND
DECORATION
4 tablespoons apricot jam
350 g/12 oz marzipan
marzipan fruits, to decorate

Grease and base-line two 20 cm/8 inch sandwich tins.

Beat the flour, baking powder, sugar, margarine and eggs until light and fluffy. Place half the mixture in one of the tins. Colour the remaining mixture pink with red food colouring. Place in the other tin. Smooth the tops and bake in a preheated oven for 30-35 minutes, until golden and firm. Leave the cakes in the tins 1 minute, then turn out on to a wire tray to cool.

Cut out a 10 cm/4 inch circle from the centre of each cake. Spread a little apricot jam around the side of each circle. Place the pink circle in the plain cake and vice versa. Sandwich the cakes together with apricot jam. Spread the remaining jam over the top and sides of the cake.

Roll out half the marzipan to cover the top of the cake. Use the remaining marzipan to cover the sides. Pinch the join at the top edge to form a decorative border. Place some marzipan fruits around the top edge, sticking with a little jam.

COOK'S TIP

Try to buy the marzipan fruits from a shop which has a quick turnover; marzipan tends to dry out once it has been made for several weeks.

180 PANFORTE DE SIENA

Preparation time:
about 25 minutes

Cooking time:
about 55 minutes

Oven temperature:
150C/300F/gas 2

Makes 1 cake

Total calories:
2855

YOU WILL NEED:
75 g/3 oz hazelnuts, toasted,
    skinned and chopped
75 g/3 oz blanched almonds,
    toasted and chopped
75 g/3 oz candied orange peel,
    chopped
75 g/3 oz candied lemon peel,
    chopped
75 g/3 oz candied fruits, chopped
2 teaspoons ground cinnamon
large pinch of mixed spice
75 g/3 oz plain flour, sifted
100 g/4 oz thick honey
90 g/3½ oz caster sugar
icing sugar, for dredging

Line a deep sandwich tin or a loose-based 18-20 cm/7-8 inch round cake tin with rice paper.

Combine the nuts, peel and fruits. Sift the spices and flour into the fruit mixture and stir until evenly mixed. Put the honey and sugar into a pan and bring slowly to the boil. Pour on to the nut mixture and stir well until blended and forming a sticky mass. Place the mixture in the tin, but not pressing it down too firmly. Bake in a preheated oven for about 50 minutes or until almost firm to the touch. Cool in the tin and then remove carefully. If the rice paper is torn or pulled away from the cake, add a new layer, attaching it with a dab of lightly beaten egg white. Dredge the top heavily with sifted icing sugar and store wrapped in foil.

COOK'S TIP

This is the Christmas cake of Siena, Italy. It is very rich and sticky so should be served cut into very small wedges or slices. If it is difficult to find the different *types of candied peel, use a good quality cut mixed peel in their place.*

181 PARIS-BREST AUX FRAISES

Preparation time: about 1 hour, plus standing	YOU WILL NEED: *1 x recipe Choux pastry (see Introduction) 1 x recipe Crème patissière (see Introduction)*
Cooking time: 45-50 minutes	*FOR THE FILLING 450 g/2 lb strawberries, all but a few hulled*
Oven temperature: 200C/400F/gas 6	*3 tablespoons orange liqueur or brandy*
Serves 10-12	*300 ml/½ pint double cream, whipped until thick*
Calories: 419-349 per portion	*icing sugar*

Grease a large baking sheet. Pipe swirls of the choux paste in a 30 cm/12 inch ring on the sheet. Bake in a preheated oven for about 40 minutes or until well risen, golden brown and firm to the touch. Turn the ring carefully over on the baking sheet and return to the oven for a few minutes for the inside to dry out. Leave to cool on a wire tray.

Reserve a few unhulled strawberries for decoration and slice the remainder. Put in a bowl with the liqueur or brandy and leave to stand for 2-4 hours. Make up the crème patissière.

Fold the cream through the crème patissière, then fold the strawberries and any juice in the bowl into the mixture.

Split the choux ring. Stand the base on a large serving dish or board. Fill with the strawberry cream and replace the lid. Dredge the top of the ring with icing sugar, if liked, and arrange the reserved strawberries on top. Serve within 2 hours.

◼ COOK'S TIP

When fresh strawberries are unavailable, or for a change, replace them with 225 g/8 oz halved and de-pipped black grapes and 2-3 sliced nectarines, soaked in the liqueur as for the strawberries. You could also use just whipped cream instead of cream and crème patissière for the filling.

182 DANISH LAYER CAKE

Preparation time: 25 minutes	YOU WILL NEED: *4 large eggs, separated grated lemon rind*
Cooking time: 30 minutes	*2 tablespoons lemon juice 125 g/5 oz icing sugar, sieved 75 g/3 oz plain flour*
Oven temperature: 180C/350F/gas 4	*25 g/1 oz cornflour ½ teaspoon baking powder FOR THE FILLING*
Makes 1 x 20 cm/ 8 inch round cake	*2 teaspoons powdered gelatine 600 ml/1 pint double cream 2 tablespoons caster sugar*
Total calories: 4605	*1 x 396 g/14 oz can pineapple pieces, drained and chopped 75 g/3 oz bitter chocolate, grated*

Grease and baseline a 20 cm/8 inch cake tin. Whisk the egg yolks, lemon rind and juice and sugar together until light and creamy. Whisk the egg whites until they form stiff peaks and fold into the egg yolk mixture. Turn into the tin and bake in a preheated oven for 30 minutes. Leave in the tin for 5 minutes, then turn out and cool. When cold, cut into three rounds.

Sprinkle the gelatine over 2 tablespoons cold water in a basin and leave to soften for 5 minutes. Stand the basin over a pan of boiling water and leave until the gelatine has dissolved. Remove from the heat and allow to cool slightly. Lightly whip two-thirds of the cream and beat in the gelatine and sugar. Fold in the pineapple and chocolate. Put the filling on one side until set. Spread each layer of sponge evenly with the filling and reassemble the cake. Chill for about 1 hour before serving.

◼ COOK'S TIP

This rich cake makes a delicious dessert, as well as a cake for serving with tea or coffee. Vary the fruit and liqueur to suit what you have available.

183 GATEAU PITHIVIERS

Preparation time: 20 minutes	YOU WILL NEED: 225 g/8 oz puff pastry or 1 x 368 g/13 oz packet frozen puff pastry, thawed
Cooking time: 25 minutes	100 g/4 oz blanched almonds, finely chopped
Oven temperature: 220C/425F/gas 7	75 g/3 oz caster sugar 50 g/2 oz butter, softened 2 teaspoons cornflour
Makes 1 x 20 cm/ 8 inch gâteau	2 large egg yolks 1 tablespoon rum (optional) 1 large egg, beaten
Total calories: 3142	1 tablespoon icing sugar, sieved

Roll out the pastry and cut into two circles, one 20 cm/8 inch in diameter and the other 23 cm/9 inch in diameter. Place the smaller circle on a damp baking sheet.

Mix the almonds with the sugar, butter, cornflour, egg yolks and rum, if using. Spread this mixture on the pastry to within 1.5 cm/½ inch of the edge. Brush the edge with beaten egg and place the larger pastry circle on top. Seal the edges well, trim them and knock up with the back of a knife. Make criss-cross cuts in the top of the pastry with a sharp knife. Brush all over the top of the pastry with beaten egg and bake in a preheated oven for 15 minutes.

Remove from the oven and sprinkle over the icing sugar. Return to the oven and cook for a further 10 minutes. Allow to cool on the baking sheet for 10 minutes, then move to a wire rack and leave until cold.

■ COOK'S TIP

This classic French pastry takes its name from the town of Pithiviers, where it has long been a speciality.

184 PRALINE GATEAU

Preparation time: 45 minutes	YOU WILL NEED: 100 g/4 oz caster sugar 3 eggs
Cooking time: 15-20 minutes	75 g/3 oz plain flour 40 g/1½ oz butter or margarine, melted
Oven temperature: 180C/350F/gas 4	grated rind of 1 lemon FOR THE PRALINE 100 g/4 oz split almonds
Makes 1 x 20 cm/ 8 inch gâteau	150 g/5 oz caster sugar FOR THE FILLING AND DECORATION
Total calories: 3491	300 ml/½ pint double cream

Whisk the sugar and eggs in a bowl over a pan of hot water until thick. Fold in the flour, butter and lemon rind and divide between two greased and base-lined 20 cm/8 inch sandwich tins. Bake for 15-20 minutes. Allow to cool slightly then turn out on to a wire rack.

Place the almonds and sugar in a pan and heat to melt the sugar. Cook until the sugar caramelizes and turns golden. Pour on to an oiled tin and allow to set. Crush finely.

Whip the cream and mix some with a little of the praline to sandwich the cake layers together. Spread the sides with more cream and coat with the praline. Spread the remaining cream on top and pipe around the cake edge with rosettes. Sprinkle with any remaining praline.

■ COOK'S TIP

The praline is best crushed in a polythene bag with a rolling pin. Prepared praline can be kept for several weeks in an airtight tin.

185 STRAWBERRY LAYER GATEAU

Preparation time:
25 minutes

Cooking time:
25-30 minutes

Oven temperature:
180C/350F/gas 4

**Makes 1 x 22.23
cm/8 ½-9 inch round
cake**

Total calories:
5006

YOU WILL NEED:
225 g/8 oz butter
225 g/8 oz caster sugar
4 large eggs, beaten
50 g/2 oz ground almonds
150 g/6 oz self-raising flour
FOR THE FILLING AND
DECORATION
450 g/1 lb strawberries
*300 ml/½ pint double cream,
   lightly whipped*

Grease and base line 2 x 22-23 cm/8 1/2-9 inch sandwich tins. Cream the butter and sugar until light and fluffy. Gradually beat in the eggs, adding a tablespoon of the almonds with the last amount. Sieve in the flour and fold into the mixture with the remaining almonds.

Turn into the prepared tins and bake in a preheated oven for 25-30 minutes or until the cakes are golden brown. Leave in the tins for 2-3 minutes, then turn out on to a wire rack and allow to cool.

Halve or quarter the strawberries, depending on size. Spread one-third of the cream and half the strawberries on one of the sponges. Sandwich the cakes together and spread half the remaining cream on top; use the remainder to pipe rosettes all round the edge. Decorate with the remaining strawberries.

◼ COOK'S TIP

The baked layers for the cake will keep well in a tin for 2-3 days before filling and decorating.

186 NOUGATINE MERINGUE

Preparation time:
50 minutes

Cooking time:
40 minutes

Oven temperature:
160C/325F/gas 3

**Makes 1 x 30 cm/
12 inch slice**

Total calories:
5785

YOU WILL NEED:
200 g/7 oz stoned dates
225 g/8 oz sponge fingers
200 g/7 oz walnuts
1 teaspoon baking powder
8 egg whites
400 g/14 oz caster sugar
FOR THE DECORATION
300 ml/½ pint double cream
150 ml/¼ pint single cream
glacé cherries, halved

Roughly chop the dates, sponge fingers and walnuts into pieces about 1 cm/½ inch in size. Toss with the baking powder. Whisk the egg whites until stiff. Carefully fold in the sugar and whisk again until soft peaks form. Fold in the date mixture and spread into a 20 x 30 cm/8 x 12 inch Swiss roll tin lined with silicone paper. Bake for about 40 minutes until lightly browned. Cool in the tin.

Turn on to a wire rack, remove the paper and cut in half lengthways. Slide one half on to a plate.

Whip the creams together. Spread half on one meringue slice, then top with the second slice. Pipe or spread the remaining cream over the top and decorate with glacé cherries.

◼ COOK'S TIP

Leave a 1 cm/½ inch border around the sides when placing the meringue mixture in the tin to allow it to swell evenly during cooking.

187 RASPBERRY ICE CREAM CAKE

Preparation time:	YOU WILL NEED:
20 minutes	*3 large eggs, separated*
	4 tablespoons hot water
Cooking time:	*150 g/6 oz caster sugar*
25 minutes	*¼ teaspoon vanilla essence*
	2 teaspoons finely grated lemon rind
Oven temperature:	*150 g/6 oz plain flour*
200C/400F/gas 6	*50 g/2 oz cornflour*
	3 teaspoons baking powder
Makes 1 x 23 cm/	*FOR THE FILLING AND TOPPING*
9 inch round cake	*1 litre/2 pints dairy ice-cream*
	225 g/8 oz fresh raspberries
Total calories:	*icing sugar, sieved*
3765	

Well grease and base line a 23 cm/9 inch cake tin.

Whisk the egg yolks with the water, sugar, vanilla essence and lemon rind until the mixture is thick and creamy. Sieve together the flour, cornflour and baking powder. Whisk the egg whites until they stand in stiff peaks. Fold the flours into the egg yolk mixture, then the egg whites.

Turn into the prepared tin and bake in a preheated oven for 25 minutes or until well risen and golden brown. Leave in the tin for 5 minutes then turn out and cool on a wire rack.

Just before serving split the cake in half. Put spoonfuls of ice cream on the bottom layer and top with the raspberries. Replace the top layer of the cake and sprinkle with icing sugar. Serve as soon as possible.

▪ COOK'S TIP

This is another cake in which the filling may be varied to suit your taste. Try pistachio ice cream and kiwi fruit, mango ice cream and fresh peach slices.

188 WALNUT BRANDY MERINGUE

Preparation time:	YOU WILL NEED:
40 minutes	*4 egg whites*
	225 g/8 oz caster sugar
Cooking time:	*50 g/2 oz walnuts, finely chopped*
1-1½ hours	*FOR THE FILLING*
	50 g/2 oz plain chocolate, broken
Oven temperature:	*into pieces*
140C/275F/gas 1	*2 tablespoons brandy*
	4 egg yolks, beaten
Makes 1 x 23 cm/	*25 g/1 oz caster sugar*
9 inch gâteau	*450 ml/¾ pint double cream,*
	whipped
Total calories:	*Maltesers*
3886	

Whisk the egg whites until stiff then whisk in the sugar until thick and glossy. Fold in the walnuts and spread the mixture into two 23 cm/9 inch rounds on baking trays lined with silicone paper. Bake for 1-1½ hours until crisp. Cool on a wire rack, then peel off the paper.

Put the chocolate, brandy, egg yolks and sugar in a bowl over a pan of simmering water. Cook until the chocolate melts and the custard coats the back of a spoon. Leave until cold.

Fold two-thirds of the whipped cream into the chocolate mixture and use to sandwich the meringue rounds together. Place on a serving plate.

Pipe the remaining whipped cream around the edge and decorate with Maltesers.

▪ COOK'S TIP

This meringue can be decorated with candied coffee beans, small pieces of chocolate flake or chocolate-coated nuts, instead of the Maltesers.

189 AUSTRIAN ORANGE CAKE

Preparation time:
25 minutes

Cooking time:
45 minutes

Oven temperature:
180C/350F/gas 4

**Makes 1 x 23 cm/
9 inch round cake**

Total calories:
3347

YOU WILL NEED:
5 large egg yolks
100 g/4 oz caster sugar
*2 teaspoons finely grated orange
   rind*
4 tablespoons orange juice
50 g/2 oz fresh white breadcrumbs
125 g/5 oz ground almonds
3 large egg whites
egg custard (see Cook's Tip)
150 g/6 oz unsalted butter
*2 teaspoons finely grated orange
   rind*
50 g/2 oz icing sugar, sifted
about 15 split blanched almonds
1 thin slice of orange

Well grease and baseline a 23 cm/9 inch cake tin. Whisk the egg yolks, sugar and orange rind until thick and creamy, then gradually whisk in the fruit juice. Fold in the breadcrumbs and almonds. Stiffly whisk the egg whites and fold into the mixture. Turn into the prepared tin and bake in a preheated oven for 45 minutes until risen and pale golden. Leave in the tin for 5 minutes, then turn out on to a wire rack to cool.

Make the egg custard. Cream the butter and orange rind until fluffy, then gradually beat in the custard and icing sugar.

Cut the cake in half. Spread with a third of the icing, then sandwich together. Spread half the remaining icing over the top and use the remainder to pipe swirls of icing round the edge. Place an almond in each. Place a twist of orange in the centre.

■ COOK'S TIP

Egg custard: heat 50 g/2 oz sugar and 150 ml/¼ pint milk to lukewarm, then stir into 2 beaten egg yolks in a heatproof basin. Beat well and put into a pan of hot water and cook, stirring, until the custard thickens. Do not allow to boil. Let cool, with a circle of greaseproof paper on top to stop a skin forming.

190 HAZELNUT TORTE

Preparation time:
20 minutes

Cooking time:
30 minutes

Oven temperature:
180C/350F/gas 4

**Makes 1 x 18 cm/
7 inch round cake**

Total calories:
2720

YOU WILL NEED:
100 g/4 oz hazelnuts
4 large eggs, separated,
125 g/5 oz caster sugar
FOR THE FILLING
50 g/2 oz unsalted butter
50 g/2 oz icing sugar, sieved
25 g/1 oz plain chocolate
FOR THE TOPPING
75 g/3 oz granulated sugar
3 tablespoons water
8 hazelnuts

Grease and line 2 x 18 cm/7 inch sandwich tins. Grind the hazelnuts. Whisk the egg yolks and sugar until thick and creamy. Whisk the egg whites until they form stiff peaks. Fold the ground nuts and egg whites alternately into the egg yolks.

Divide the mixture between the tins and bake in a preheated oven for 30 minutes or until set. Leave the cakes in the tins for 10 minutes, then turn out on to a wire rack to cool.

Cream the butter and beat in the icing sugar. Melt the chocolate in a basin over a pan of hot water. Beat into the butter and sugar. Spread the filling over one of the cakes and sandwich the other one on top.

Put the sugar and water into a pan and heat gently until the sugar has melted, then boil rapidly until a golden caramel is reached. Using an oiled knife, spread the caramel evenly over the top of the cake. While it is still soft mark into portions with the point of a knife and place the hazelnuts in position.

■ COOK'S TIP

Give the blender or grinder just a couple of pulses to grind the hazelnuts finely. Do not reduce them to a powder.

191 BRANDY AND ORANGE GATEAU

Preparation time: 40 minutes	YOU WILL NEED: *2 eggs* *50 g/2 oz caster sugar*
Cooking time: about 30 minutes	*50 g/2 oz plain flour* *grated rind of 1 orange* *1 quantity Barnstaple gingerbread*
Oven temperature: 180C/350F/gas 4	*mixture (recipe 224)* *300 ml/½ pint double cream* *3 tablespoons brandy*
Serves 6	
Calories: 435 per portion	

Grease and base line 2 x 18 cm/7 inch sandwich tins. Whisk the eggs and sugar in a bowl until light and thick. Sift the flour into the bowl and fold into the mixture, with half the orange rind. Divide the mixture between the tins and bake in a preheated oven for 20 minutes, until light golden and firm to the touch. Turn out the cakes and cool on a wire tray.

Make the gingerbread (see Cook's Tip). Whisk the cream and brandy until stiff. Stir in the remaining orange rind.

Spread one cake with a little cream. Sprinkle on some broken biscuits and place the other cake on top. Spread cream round the side of the cake and roll in the remaining biscuits. Spread the top with a little cream. Fill the cones with cream and place on top of the cake, radiating from the centre. Pipe cream rosettes round the edge of the cake and 1 in the centre.

COOK'S TIP

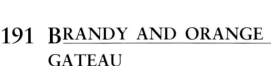

Make the gingerbread biscuits as in recipe 224. While still warm , shape 6 biscuits into cones. When the rest are cold, break into small pieces.

192 STRAWBERRY CREAM GATEAU

Preparation time: 20 minutes	YOU WILL NEED: *3 eggs* *75 g/3 oz caster sugar*
Cooking time: 20-25 minutes	*75 g/3 oz plain flour* *25 g/1 oz butter, melted* FOR THE FILLING AND
Oven temperature: 180C/350F/gas 4	DECORATION *300 ml/½ pint double or* *whipping cream*
Makes 1 x 20 cm/ 8 inch cake	*350 g/12 oz strawberries* *2 tablespoons redcurrant jelly*
Total calories: 2497	

Grease and line 2 x 20 cm/8 inch sandwich tins.

Whisk the eggs and sugar together until the mixture is light and thick and leaves a trail when the whisk is lifted from it. Sift the flour into the bowl and fold in lightly, until evenly mixed. Pour the melted butter slowly into the mixture and fold in. Pour into the prepared tins, level the tops and bake in a preheated oven 20-25 minutes until the cake is golden brown and firm to touch. Turn out and cool on a wire tray.

Whip the cream till stiff; slice half the strawberries. Spread a third of the cream over 1 cake and cover with the sliced strawberries and the other cake. Spread half the remaining cream over the top. Cut the remaining strawberries in half and place on top. Warm the jelly and brush over the strawberries. Pipe rosettes of cream around the edge of the cake.

COOK'S TIP

Try this gâteau with any other colourful fruit in season. Blackberries, peach slices, dessert plums, halved, or kiwi fruit are all suitable. To glaze the

lighter coloured fruits, replace the redcurrant jelly with warmed, sieved apricot jam.

193 INDIVIDUAL BIRTHDAY CAKE

Preparation time: 20 minutes	YOU WILL NEED: *50 g/2 oz butter or margarine* *50 g/2 oz caster sugar*
Cooking time: 50-60 minutes	*few drops of vanilla essence* *1 egg* *75 g/3 oz self-raising flour*
Oven temperature: 160C/325F/gas 3	FOR THE ICING AND DECORATION *1 gold doily*
Makes 1 x 9 cm/ 3½ inch cake	*piece of ribbon* *50 g/2 oz icing sugar, sifted* *2 teaspoons water*
Total calories: 1256	*slice of citron peel*

Cream the butter with the sugar and vanilla essence until pale and fluffy. Gradually beat in the egg then sift the flour over the mixture and fold in gently. Spoon into a greased and lined 9 cm/3½ inch round tin, about 10 cm/4 inch deep. Bake for 50-60 minutes, then turn out to cool on a wire rack.

To ice and decorate the cake, fold a doily around the cake and tie a ribbon around it. Mix the icing sugar with the water to give a thick icing. Spoon on top of the cake and decorate with a slice of citron peel. Leave to set.

194 SNOW-PEAKED CAKE

Preparation time: Make 2-3 months in advance	YOU WILL NEED: *1 x 20 cm/8 inch round Rich celebration cake (see recipe 159)* FOR THE ICING AND
Cooking time: 3½ hours	DECORATION *550 g/1¼ lb Almond paste (see Introduction)*
Oven temperature: 150C/300F/gas 2	*23 cm/9 inch round silver cake board* *675 g/1½ lb Royal icing*
Makes 1 x 20 cm/ 8 inch round cake	*(see Introduction)* *Christmas cake decorations ribbon*
Total calories: 12537	

Make the cake as directed, bake and leave to mature for 2-3 months. Cover with Almond paste, 1-2 weeks before icing and place on the silver cake board.

Flat ice the sides of the cake with the Royal icing then rough ice the top (see Cook's Tip). Decorate with Christmas cake decorations - a Father Christmas, snowman, robin, reindeer, snow-covered post box or angels, for example. Tie a ribbon around the cake to complete.

■ COOK'S TIP

To ensure that a white glacé icing does not become grey, sift the icing sugar through a nylon, not metal, sieve.

■ COOK'S TIP

To rough ice the top of the cake, cover the top completely with icing and smooth evenly. Then, using the tip of a palette knife, dip it into the icing and press the tip of the knife on to the surface of the icing and draw away to form a peak. Repeat this process until the top of the cake is covered in peaks of icing.

195 GATEAU DIANE

Preparation time: 30 minutes	YOU WILL NEED: *4 egg whites* *225 g/8 oz caster sugar*
Cooking time: 1½-2 hours	FOR THE FILLING AND DECORATION *1 recipe chocolate Butter icing*
Oven temperature: 140C/275F/gas 1	*(see Introduction)* *50 g/2 oz flaked almonds, toasted* *25 g/1 oz plain chocolate, melted*
Makes 1 x 20 cm/ 8 inch gâteau	
Total calories: 2877	

Whisk the egg whites until stiff, then add 2 tablespoons of the sugar and continue whisking until the mixture is very stiff. Carefully fold in the remaining sugar. Spoon into mounds or pipe into two 20 cm/8 inch rounds on baking trays lined with silicone paper. Bake for 1½-2 hours until crisp. Peel off the lining paper and cool on a wire rack.

Sandwich the meringue rounds together with one-third of the chocolate butter icing. Spread the remaining butter icing on top of the meringue and around the sides. Sprinkle almonds over the top. Put the melted chocolate in a greaseproof paper piping bag, snip off the end and drizzle lines of chocolate over the nuts.

196 STRAWBERRY TORTE

Preparation time: 1 hour	YOU WILL NEED: *1½ recipes Victoria sandwich mixture (see recipe 93)*
Cooking time: 25-30 minutes	*1 kg/2 lb strawberries, hulled* *600 ml/1 pint double cream, whipped*
Oven temperature: 180C/350F/gas 4	*6 tablespoons sweet or medium sherry* *3 tablespoons granulated sugar*
Makes 1 x 23 cm/ 9 inch gâteau	*1½ teaspoons cornflour* *2 tablespoons water* *1 teaspoon lemon juice*
Total calories: 5942	*100 g/4 oz toasted flaked almonds*

Divide the cake mixture between three greased and lined 23 cm/9 inch sandwich tins. Bake for 25-30 minutes then turn out to cool on a wire rack.

Purée 225 g/8 oz of the strawberries and slice 225 g/8 oz. Sieve the puréed strawberries and fold into 450 ml/¾ pint whipped cream with the sliced strawberries. Sprinkle the cake layers with the sherry then sandwich together with the prepared cream.

Purée 175 g/6 oz of the remaining strawberries, sieve and place in a pan with the sugar, cornflour and water. Cook for 1-2 minutes until thickened. Stir in the lemon juice and cool. Halve the remaining strawberries and place, cut sides down, on top of the cake. Brush with the glaze to coat. Brush the sides of the cake with the glaze and coat with the almonds. Pipe the edge of the cake with the remaining whipped cream.

◼ COOK'S TIP

Put the broken chocolate in the piping bag and cook in a microwave on Medium (50%) power for 1½-2½ minutes until melted. Snip off the end and pipe.

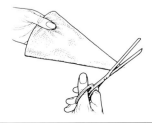

◼ COOK'S TIP

When strawberries are expensive, use 675 g/1½ lb. Glaze the strawberries and sides of the cake with sieved strawberry or raspberry jam thinned with a little water and lemon juice. Heat until bubbly before use.

BISCUITS & COOKIES

Here are biscuits and cookies to suit all tastes, from such traditional plain fare as Digestive biscuits and Peanut cookies to biscuits laden with chocolate chips, glacé fruits and nuts. Most of them are quite quick to prepare and bake, so there's no excuse for empty biscuits tins or cookie jars in the kitchen cupboard.

197 FLORENTINES

Preparation time:	YOU WILL NEED:
20 minutes	50 g/2 oz butter
	50 g/2 oz demerara sugar
Cooking time:	1 tablespoon golden syrup
12-15 minutes	50 g/2 oz glacé cherries, chopped
	25 g/1 oz walnuts, chopped
Oven temperature:	25 g/1 oz sultanas
190C/375F/gas 5	25 g/1 oz chopped mixed peel
	25 g/1 oz plain flour
Makes 18-20	50 g/2 oz flaked almonds
	1 teaspoon lemon juice
Calories:	100 g/4 oz plain chocolate, melted
112-101 per portion	

Put the butter, sugar and syrup in a saucepan. Heat gently until the butter has melted and the sugar has dissolved. Add the remaining ingredients, except the chocolate and mix well.

Place teaspoonfuls of the mixture, leaving plenty of space for the mixture to spread, on greased baking trays. Bake for 12-15 minutes, until well spread and golden brown.

Leave for 1 minute, then transfer to a wire rack using a palette knife and cool completely. Spread the base of each with the melted chocolate, making wavy lines with a fork. Leave on the wire rack to set.

198 BRANDY SNAP CREAMS

Preparation time:	YOU WILL NEED:
20 minutes	50 g/2 oz butter or margarine
	1 tablespoon golden syrup
Cooking time:	50 g/2 oz soft brown sugar
about 30 minutes	1 teaspoon lemon juice
	50 g/2 oz plain flour
Oven temperature:	1 teaspoon ground ginger
180C/350F/gas 4	½ teaspoon ground mixed spice
	300 ml/½ pint double cream
Makes about 20	25 g/1 oz stem ginger, very finely
	chopped
Calories:	1 teaspoon brandy or ginger wine
118 per portion	(optional)
	2 tablespoons chopped mixed nuts

Melt the butter in a pan with the golden syrup and sugar. When bubbling, add the lemon juice, flour, ginger and mixed spice, mixing well. Place teaspoonfuls on to a greased baking tray, allowing room to spread.

Bake, in batches, for 6-8 minutes. Cool slightly, lift with a spatula and while hot, mould around the greased handles of wooden spoons. Cool then remove.

Whip the cream with the stem ginger and brandy or ginger wine if used. Fill the brandy snaps with the cream and dip the ends into nuts to coat. Chill lightly before serving.

■ COOK'S TIP

Break chocolate into small squares so that it melts evenly. Put it into a heatproof bowl over a pan of hot water and heat gently, stirring frequently.

Never melt chocolate over direct heat.

■ COOK'S TIP

The brandy snaps can also be moulded around cream horn tins. The cream can then be piped or spooned into the open end and dipped in nuts for serving.

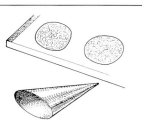

199 AMARETTI

Preparation time:	YOU WILL NEED:
20 minutes	*100 g/4 oz ground almonds*
	15 g/½ oz ground rice or rice flour
Cooking time:	*225 g/8 oz caster sugar*
about 20 minutes	*¼ teaspoon ratafia essence*
	2 egg whites
Oven temperature:	*2 sheets of rice paper*
180C/350F/gas 4	*12 blanched almonds, split*
	1 beaten egg white, to glaze
Makes 24	
Calories:	
66 per portion	

Mix together the ground almonds, ground rice or rice flour and sugar. Add the ratafia essence to the unbeaten egg whites and mix into the dry ingredients. Cream to a smooth paste.

Place the mixture in a piping bag with a plain 1 cm/½ inch nozzle. Rule the rice paper into 5 cm/2 inch squares. Pipe the mixture into the centre of each square, making biscuits 2.5 cm/1 inch in diameter; flatten slightly. Press a split almond in the centre of each and brush lightly with beaten egg white.

Bake for about 20 minutes, or until golden brown. Cool on a wire tray and trim the rice paper round each biscuit. Store in an airtight container.

▧ COOK'S TIP

These Italian biscuits are made in various sizes. Small ones are used for petits fours and for decoration; larger ones are crushed and added to dessert creams.

200 DATE PINWHEEL COOKIES

Preparation time:	YOU WILL NEED:
30 minutes, plus	*FOR THE FILLING*
chilling	*100 g/4 oz dates, stoned and*
	chopped
Cooking time:	*3 oz/75 g caster sugar*
10-12 minutes	*125 ml/¼ pint water*
	25 g/1 oz blanched almonds, finely
Oven temperature:	*chopped*
190C/375F/gas 5	*FOR THE SHORTBREAD*
	100 g/4 oz self-raising flour
Makes about 30	*¼ teaspoon salt*
	¼ teaspoon baking powder
Calories:	*50 g/2 oz butter*
67 per portion	*75 g/3 oz caster sugar*
	1 egg yolk

Put the dates in a pan with the sugar and the water. Simmer over low heat until the mixture thickens. Remove from the heat, cool, then stir in the almonds. Sift the flour, salt and baking powder. Cream the butter and sugar. Beat in the egg yolk, then stir in the flour. Knead to a smooth dough, wrap in greaseproof paper or foil and chill for 1 hour.

Roll out the dough on a floured surface to a rectangle about 20 x 35 cm/8 x 14 inches. Spoon the date mixture over and spread evenly. Roll up the dough like a Swiss roll, starting at a short side. Wrap in greaseproof paper or foil and chill for 3-4 hours. Cut the roll into 6 mm/¼ inch thick slices. Place on well-greased baking tray and bake for 10-12 minutes or until golden. After a minute, remove with a palette knife and cool on a wire rack.

▧ COOK'S TIP

Some biscuits and cookies spread considerably during cooking: leave plenty of space between them when putting the mixture on greased baking trays.

201 CINNAMON AND ALMOND SLICES

Preparation time:
15 minutes

Cooking time:
20 minutes

Oven temperature:
180C/350F/gas 4

Makes 18

Calories:
92 per portion

YOU WILL NEED:
100 g/4 oz butter
50 g/2 oz caster sugar
150 g/5 oz plain flour
½ teaspoon ground cinnamon
a little beaten egg, to glaze
25 g/1 oz flaked almonds
1 tablespoon granulated sugar

Grease a 28 x 18 cm/11 x 7 inch Swiss roll tin thoroughly. Cream the butter and caster sugar together until light and fluffy. Sift the flour and cinnamon and work well into the butter and sugar mixture.

Press the mixture into the prepared tin and flatten with a palette knife. Brush with a little beaten egg and prick lightly with a fork. Sprinkle with the almonds and granulated sugar.

Bake for 20 minutes or until golden brown. Cool in the tin and mark into fingers while still warm.

202 GINGER BISCUITS

Preparation time:
10-15 minutes

Cooking time:
20 minutes

Oven temperature:
190C/375F/gas 5

Makes 12-14

Calories:
199-170 per portion

YOU WILL NEED:
225 g/8 oz plain flour
1 teaspoon ground ginger
100 g/4 oz butter or margarine
100 g/4 oz molasses sugar
100 g/4 oz cane syrup

Sift the flour with the ginger. Cream the butter with the sugar until light and fluffy. Add the flour mixture with the cane syrup and knead until smooth.

Roll out on a floured surface and stamp out rounds using a 7.5 cm/3 inch cutter. Place on greased baking trays.

Bake for 20 minutes, then transfer to a wire rack to cool.

▨ COOK'S TIP

Home-made biscuits and cookies are a good standby for the store cupboard as they will keep well for at least a week if stored in an airtight container.

▨ COOK'S TIP

This mixture is enough to make 6-7 gingerbread men. Use a cutter and make buttons for eyes and mouths from raisins and slivers of glacé cherries.

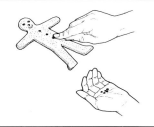

203 BUTTER SHORTBREAD

Preparation time:
15-20 minutes

Cooking time:
30-35 minutes

Oven temperature:
170C/325F/gas 3

Makes 8-10

Calories:
207-166 per portion

YOU WILL NEED:
100 g/4 oz plain four
50 g/2 oz cornflour
50 g/2 oz caster sugar
100 g/4 oz butter

Sift together the flour and cornflour. Add the sugar and rub in the butter. The mixture will become crumbly at first but continue rubbing in with your fingers until it clings together in heavy lumps.

Turn on to a board or working surface lightly dusted with flour or cornflour and knead lightly. Roll out to a 20 cm/8 inch circle and place on a greased baking tray. Prick all over the top with a fork, mark into eight or ten portions and flute the edges with your fingers.

Bake for 30-35 minutes until the shortbread is cooked but not browned. Leave on the baking tray for 10 minutes, then lift off with a fish slice and place carefully on a wire rack to cool.

204 PEANUT COOKIES

Preparation time:
20 minutes

Cooking time:
12 minutes

Oven temperature:
180C/350F/gas 4

Makes about 20

Calories:
about 94 per portion

YOU WILL NEED:
100 g/4 oz butter or margarine
50 g/2 oz caster sugar
150 g/5 oz plain flour
pinch of salt
a little milk
50 g/2 oz peanuts, roughly chopped

Cream the butter or margarine and sugar until light and fluffy. Sift the flour and salt together, stir into the mixture and mix to a stiff dough.

Turn on to a floured surface, knead lightly and roll out to a 6 mm/¼ inch thickness. Cut into circles with a 5 cm/2 inch cutter and place on greased baking trays. Brush the biscuits with milk and sprinkle with the chopped nuts.

Bake for about 12 minutes or until crisp and golden brown. Leave on the trays for a minute, then remove and cool on a wire rack.

■ COOK'S TIP

This basic recipe can be varied in many ways by adding, for example, finely grated orange or lemon rind, chocolate chips or finely chopped almonds.

■ COOK'S TIP

Once opened, packets of nuts can become rancid quite quickly. It is best to store nuts in an airtight container in the refrigerator.

205 CINNAMON SHORTBREAD

Preparation time:
15 minutes, plus 1
hour chilling time

Cooking time:
40 minutes

Oven temperature:
160C/325F/gas 3

Makes 8

Calories:
207 per portion

YOU WILL NEED:
150 g/5 oz plain flour
pinch of salt
1 teaspoon ground cinnamon
25 g/1 oz ground rice
50 g/2 oz caster sugar
10 g/4 oz butter
caster sugar, to dust

Sift the flour, salt, cinnamon and rice into a bowl and stir in the sugar. Rub in the butter then knead until smooth but not sticky. Wrap in clingfilm and chill for 30 minutes.

Press the dough out to an 18 cm/7 inch round and place on a greased baking tray. Flute the edge and prick all over with a fork. Mark into 8 portions and chill for 30 minutes.

Bake for about 40 minutes or until pale golden. Leave on the baking tray for 10 minutes, then transfer to a wire rack to cool. Dust with sugar to serve.

206 ANZAC COOKIES

Preparation time:
20 minutes

Cooking time:
20 minutes

Oven temperature:
170C/325F/gas 3

Makes about 30

Calories:
33 per portion

YOU WILL NEED:
2 tablespoons golden syrup
125 g/4½ oz butter
100 g/4 oz caster sugar
100 g/4 oz plain flour
75 g/3 oz rolled oats
50 g/2 oz desiccated coconut
2 teaspoons bicarbonate of soda
1 tablespoon hot water

Put the syrup, butter and sugar in a saucepan and heat gently until the butter has melted and the sugar dissolved. Remove from the heat, sift in the flour, add the oats and coconut and beat well. Dissolve the bicarbonate of soda in the water and add to the mixture in the pan.

When the mixture is cool enough to handle, roll into about 30 small balls and place on greased baking trays, allowing plenty of room for the cookies to spread.

Bake for 20 minutes or until the cookies are an even golden brown. Leave on the baking trays for a minute or two, then place on wire racks to cool.

■ COOK'S TIP

The mixture can be pressed into a decorative shortbread mould. Dust it liberally with caster sugar, to make unmoulding the mixture on to the baking tray easier.

■ COOK'S TIP

Biscuits containing syrup or honey are usually still soft when taken from the oven. Leave them in the tin or on the tray for a few minutes to allow them to crisp *before transferring them to a wire rack to cool.*

207 DIGESTIVE BISCUITS

Preparation time:
15 minutes

Cooking time:
15-20 minutes

Oven temperature:
190C/375F/gas 5

Makes about 22

Calories:
69 per portion

YOU WILL NEED:
175 g/6 oz wholemeal flour
25 g/1 oz medium oatmeal
½ teaspoon salt
1 teaspoon baking powder
75 g/3 oz butter or margarine
40 g/1½ oz soft brown sugar
2-3 tablespoons milk

Mix the flour and oatmeal together, then sift in the salt and baking powder. Rub in the butter, then stir in the sugar. Add the milk and mix to a soft dough. Roll out thinly on a floured surface, prick well and cut into 6 cm/2½ inch rounds with a plain cutter. Place on greased baking trays.

Bake for 15-20 minutes then cool on a wire rack.

208 BROWN BISCUITS

Preparation time:
20 minutes, plus
chilling

Cooking time:
10 minutes

Oven temperature:
200C/400F/gas 6

Makes about 36

Calories:
about 69 per portion

YOU WILL NEED:
100 g/4 oz butter
100 g/4 oz caster sugar
50 g/2 oz golden syrup
25 g/1 oz blanched almonds, finely
  chopped
25 g/1 oz chopped mixed peel
225 g/8 oz plain flour
½ teaspoon ground cloves
1 teaspoon ground cinnamon
¼ teaspoon ground ginger

Put the butter, sugar and syrup in a pan and heat gently until the butter has melted and the sugar dissolved. Remove from the heat and add the almonds and peel. Allow to cool, then sift in the flour with the spices; mix well.

Using your hands, roll the dough into a sausage about 6 cm/2 inches in diameter. Wrap in greaseproof paper and chill for a few hours or overnight.

Remove the greaseproof paper and cut the dough into paper-thin slices. Place on greased baking trays and bake for 10 minutes or until crisp. Leave on the baking trays for a minute, then remove with a palette knife and cool on a wire tray.

◼ COOK'S TIP

Coat these digestives with a little melted chocolate after cooling. You will need about 150 g/5 oz melted chocolate to spread on one side of the biscuits.

◼ COOK'S TIP

To blanch almonds, pour boiling water over them and leave for 2 minutes. Drain and cover with cold water. Rub the skins off with your fingers. Almonds will be juicier if not blanched until just before they are needed.

209 DATE AND WALNUT CRISPIES

Preparation time:	YOU WILL NEED:
15 minutes	100 g/4 oz lard or cooking fat
	1 egg
Cooking time:	100 g/4 oz caster sugar
about 40 minutes	225 g/8 oz dates, pitted and
	chopped
Oven temperature:	50 g/2 oz walnuts, chopped
180C/350F/gas 4	100 g/4 oz self-raising flour
	pinch of salt
Makes about 20	sifted icing sugar, to coat
Calories:	
about 140 per	
portion	

Grease an 18 cm/7 inch shallow square cake tin thoroughly.

Melt the lard or cooking fat and allow to cool slightly. Beat the egg and sugar together until light and fluffy. Add the lard or fat, dates and walnuts and mix well. Sift in the flour and salt and beat well. Turn the mixture into the prepared tin and spread out evenly.

Bake for about 40 minutes or until golden brown and well risen. Remove from the oven and allow to cool for 10 minutes in the tin before cutting into small squares. When cold, remove from the tin and roll in icing sugar to coat.

210 CRUNCHY DATE LAYER

Preparation time:	YOU WILL NEED:
20 minutes	FOR THE FILLING
	225 g/8 oz dates, pitted and
	chopped
Cooking time:	2 tablespoons water
25-30 minutes	1 tablespoon lemon juice
	1 tablespoon honey
Oven temperature:	pinch of ground cinnamon
180C/350F/gas 4	FOR THE OAT MIXTURE
Makes 14 fingers	100 g/4 oz wholemeal flour
	150 g/5 oz rolled oats
Calories:	225 g/8 oz butter
233 per portion	

Grease an 18 cm/7 inch shallow square cake tin thoroughly.

Put the dates and water in a pan and simmer gently until the dates are soft. Allow to cool, then stir in the lemon juice, honey and cinnamon.

Mix the flour and oats in a mixing bowl; rub in the butter. Divide this mixture in half. Press half into the bottom of the prepared tin. Spread with the date mixture and cover with the remaining oat mixture.

Bake for 20-25 minutes. Cool in the tin and cut into 14 fingers while still warm. Remove from the tin carefully when quite cold.

■ COOK'S TIP

If an egg is stuck in the carton, immerse the carton in cold water for a few minutes and then you will be able to remove the egg without cracking the shell.

■ COOK'S TIP

If a lemon has been stored in the refrigerator, bring it to room temperature before squeezing to obtain the maximum amount of juice. A juicy lemon yields about *45 ml/3 tablespoons of juice.*

211 OATMEAL AND CHOCOLATE CHIP COOKIES

Preparation time:
15 minutes

Cooking time:
12-15 minutes

Oven temperature:
180C/350F/gas 4

Makes about 36

Calories:
about 68 per portion

YOU WILL NEED:
100 g/4 oz butter or margarine
100 g/4 oz caster sugar
1 egg, beaten
½ teaspoon vanilla essence
75 g/3 oz plain flour
pinch of salt
40 g/1½ oz rolled oats
100 g/4 oz chocolate chips

Cream the butter or margarine and sugar together until light and fluffy. Gradually beat in the egg and vanilla essence. Sift in the flour and salt. Fold into the creamed mixture together with the oats and chocolate chips.

Drop teaspoons of the mixture on to very well-greased baking trays. Bake for 12-15 minutes or until very lightly browned. Leave on the baking trays for a minute, then remove with a palette knife and cool on wire racks.

212 FLAPJACKS

Preparation time:
5-10 minutes

Cooking time:
25-30 minutes

Oven temperature:
180C/350F/gas 4

Makes 16

Calories:
150 per portion

YOU WILL NEED:
100 g/4 oz butter or margarine
100 g/4 oz soft brown sugar
3 tablespoons golden syrup
225 g/8 oz rolled oats

Melt the butter with the sugar and syrup in a large pan. Stir in the rolled oats and mix thoroughly. Turn the mixture into a greased 20 cm/8 inch shallow, square tin and smooth the top with a palette knife.

Bake for 25-30 minutes until golden brown. Cut into slices while still warm, then cool completely before removing from the tin.

▦ COOK'S TIP

Unless you have a very large oven, you will probably find that you will need to bake these cookies in two separate batches.

▦ COOK'S TIP

Try coating the flapjacks with a sesame topping. Mix 50 g/2 oz sesame seeds with 2 tablespoons thick honey and warm to a spreading consistency. Spread over the flapjack mixture after baking, return to the oven for a further 5-10 minutes.

213 MACAROONS

Preparation time:
15 minutes

Cooking time:
20-25 minutes

Oven temperature:
180C/350F/gas 4

Makes 10

Calories:
97 per portion

YOU WILL NEED:
100 g/4 oz ground almonds
100 g/4 oz caster sugar
2 egg whites
½ teaspoon almond essence
rice paper, to line
10 whole almonds

Mix together the ground almonds and sugar. Whisk the egg whites until stiff. Fold the almond mixture and almond essence into the egg whites.

Place the mixture in a piping bag fitted with a large plain tube. Pipe ten rounds about 5 cm/2 inches across on to a baking tray lined with rice paper. Press an almond into the centre of each.

Bake for 20-25 minutes, until lightly browned and firm. Remove from the baking tray and cool on a wire rack, then trim off the extra rice paper.

214 CHERRY AND NUT CRINKLES

Preparation time:
15 minutes

Cooking time:
7-8 minutes

Oven temperature:
190C/375F/gas 5

Makes 10-12

Calories:
106-88 per portion

YOU WILL NEED:
50 g/2 oz butter
50 g/2 oz caster sugar
40 g/1½ oz plain flour, sifted
50 g/2 oz glacé cherries, coarsely
  chopped
50 g/2 oz flaked almonds

Beat the butter and sugar together until creamy. Work in the flour and cherries and then the flaked almonds.

Drop teaspoonfuls of the mixture on to a greased baking tray - about 7.5 cm/3 inches apart to allow for spreading. Bake for 7-8 minutes until golden brown. Allow to cool slightly, then remove from the baking tray with a palette knife and cool on a wire rack.

Store in an airtight tin or plastic container.

■ COOK'S TIP

Rice paper, made from the pith of an Oriental tree, is available from some delicatessens, Oriental food shops and specialist cake decorating suppliers.

■ COOK'S TIP

These delicious thin and crunchy biscuits can be varied by substituting coarsely chopped walnuts for the almonds and chopped candied orange *peel for the glacé cherries.*

215 JAM FACES

Preparation time:
20 minutes

Cooking time:
15 minutes

Oven temperature:
190C/375F/gas 5

Makes about 20

Calories:
216 per portion

YOU WILL NEED:
225 g/8 oz butter or margarine
225 g/8 oz caster sugar
2 eggs, beaten
few drops of vanilla essence
450 g/1 lb plain flour, sifted
jam for spreading

Cream the butter with the sugar, then gradually beat in the eggs and vanilla essence. Stir in the flour and mix to a fairly soft dough. Turn onto a floured surface and knead gently. Roll out to 3 mm/⅛ inch thickness and cut into rounds with a 6 cm/2½ inch cutter. From half of these, remove two mounds to represent eyes, using a 1 cm/½ inch cutter, then make a slit for the mouth.

Place all the biscuits on greased baking trays.

Bake for about 15 minutes or until golden. Leave the biscuits on the baking trays for a few minutes, then transfer to a wire rack to cool.

When cold, spread the plain biscuits with jam and put the faces on top.

216 DUTCH MOPPEN

Preparation time:
20 minutes

Cooking time:
about 10 minutes

Oven temperature:
190C/375F/gas 5

Makes 12

Calories:
149 per portion

YOU WILL NEED:
100 g/4 oz butter
75 g/3 oz caster sugar
125 g/4½ oz self-raising flour,
    sifted
6 blanched almonds
1 beaten egg, to glaze

Cream the butter and sugar together until smooth. Work in the flour. Knead on a floured board into a large ball, working in a little more flour if it is too greasy.

Scoop off small pieces with a teaspoon and roll into walnut-sized balls. Place on a greased baking tray at least 5 cm/2 inches apart to allow for spreading. Flatten the balls slightly. Split the almonds in two and press a half in the centre of each cookie. Brush the tops with beaten egg.

Bake in the centre of the oven for about 10 minutes or until golden. Lift the biscuits off the baking tray with a palette knife and cool on a wire rack. Store in an airtight tin or plastic container.

▨ COOK'S TIP

These make a welcome addition to a child's birthday party menu. Children will especially enjoy cutting out the faces - try varying the shapes of
the eyes and mouths for extra fun.

▨ COOK'S TIP

These crisp butter cookies are also ideal to serve with ice cream or after-dinner coffee. Walnut halves can be used instead of the blanched almonds.

217 WHEATMEAL BISCUITS

Preparation time:
15-20 minutes

Cooking time:
about 15 minutes

Oven temperature:
180C/350F/gas 4

Makes about 24

Calories:
about 84 per portion

YOU WILL NEED:
225 g/8 oz wholemeal flour
pinch of salt
25 g/1 oz granulated sugar
150 g/5 oz butter or margarine
1 egg, beaten

Mix the flour, salt and sugar together. Cut the fat into the flour and rub in to obtain a breadcrumb consistency. Stir in the beaten egg and knead into a stiff dough. (If the egg is small you may need a teaspoon of water.)

Roll out thinly on a board sprinkled with wheatmeal flour and cut into round biscuits with a plain cutter. Place on a greased baking tray. Work up, roll and cut out the trimmings.

Bake for about 5 minutes or until crisp and golden. Cool on a wire rack and store in an airtight container.

218 OAT BISCUITS

Preparation time:
15-20 minutes

Cooking time:
15 minutes

Oven temperature:
180C/350F/gas 4

Makes about 24

Calories:
76 per portion

YOU WILL NEED:
100 g/4 oz flour
½ teaspoon salt
100 g/4 oz rolled oats
50 g/2 oz caster sugar
65 g/2½ oz lard or margarine
1 egg, beaten
2-3 tablespoons milk

Sift the flour and salt into a mixing bowl. Mix in the rolled oats and sugar. Cut the fat into the mixture, then rub in with the fingertips to a breadcrumb consistency. Bind with the beaten egg, adding a little milk as necessary to make a stiff dough.

Roll out thinly on a floured board. Using a plain cutter, cut out 7 cm/2½ inch rounds. Place on a greased baking tray. Work up, roll and cut out the scraps.

Bake for 15 minutes, or until crisp and golden. Cool on a wire rack.

▥ COOK'S TIP

These slightly sweet biscuits are an ideal accompaniment to cream cheese. They can, if preferred, be made with soft brown sugar instead of white.

▥ COOK'S TIP

To make chocolate-covered oat biscuits coat one side with chocolate Glacé Icing (see Introduction) when they are cold. They can also be coated in melted chocolate - milk or plain, according to your preference.

219 GARIBALDI BISCUITS

Preparation time:	YOU WILL NEED:
20-25 minutes	*100 g/4 oz self-raising flour*
	pinch of salt
Cooking time:	*40 g/1½ oz butter or margarine*
10-12 minutes	*25 g/1 oz caster sugar*
	3 tablespoons milk
Oven temperature:	*50 g/2 oz currants*
200C/400F/gas 6	*beaten egg, to glaze*

Makes 24

Calories:
35 per portion

Sift the flour with the salt, rub in the butter then add the sugar, mixing well. Add 2 tablespoons of the milk and mix to a firm dough. Knead until smooth, about 2-3 minutes.

Roll out to a 23 cm/9 inch square, cut in half and brush one half with the remaining milk. Sprinkle evenly with the currants, then cover with the remaining piece of dough. Press down lightly to seal, then roll out with a floured rolling pin to a 25 x 20 cm/10 x 8 inch rectangle. Cut into 24 neat fingers and place on greased baking trays. Glaze with beaten egg.

Bake for 10-12 minutes or until golden. Cool slightly on the trays then on a wire rack.

220 MUESLI BARS

Preparation time:	YOU WILL NEED:
10 minutes	*3 tablespoons clear honey*
	100 g/4 oz butter
Cooking time:	*50 g/2 oz soft light brown sugar*
20 minutes	*50 g/2 oz mixed nuts, chopped*
	100 g/4 oz rolled oats
Oven temperature:	*25 g/1 oz desiccated coconut*
180C/350F/gas 4	*50 g/2 oz sesame seeds*
	100 g/4 oz plain chocolate, melted
Makes 18	*(optional)*

Calories:
173 per portion

Put the honey, butter and sugar in a saucepan. Heat gently until the butter has melted and the sugar has dissolved. Stir in the nuts, oats, coconut and sesame seeds.

Press evenly into a greased 28 x 18 cm/11 x 7 inch shallow oblong. Bake for 20 minutes until golden brown.

Cool for 5 minutes in the tin, then cut into three lengthways and six across. leave in the tin to cool completely.

Dip one end of the bar in the melted chocolate, if using.

▮ COOK'S TIP

These biscuits will keep for up to 1 week if stored in an airtight tin.

▮ COOK'S TIP

Use up leftover nuts at the end of a packet to make a ready supply of chopped mixed nuts. Keep them in an airtight container in the refrigerator.

221 CINNAMON RINGS

Preparation time:	YOU WILL NEED:
15 minutes	*175 g/6 oz plain flour*
	100 g/4 oz butter or margarine
Cooking time:	*50 g/2 oz caster sugar*
10-15 minutes	*½ teaspoon ground cinnamon*
	grated rind of 1 orange
Oven temperature:	*1 egg yolk*
180C/350F/gas 4	FOR THE DECORATION
	225 g/8 oz icing sugar, sifted
Makes 24	*2-3 tablespoons orange juice*
	coarsely grated orange rind
Calories:	
111 per portion	

Sift the flour into a bowl and rub in the butter. Add the sugar, cinnamon, orange rind and egg yolk and mix to a smooth dough. Knead lightly then roll out thinly. Use a 6 cm/2½ inch cutter to cut out 24 biscuits. Cut the middle out of each biscuit using a 2.5 cm/1 inch fluted cutter. Place on greased baking trays.

Bake for 10-15 minutes until golden then cool on a wire rack.

To decorate the rings, mix the icing sugar with the orange juice until smooth. Carefully coat the top of the biscuits with the icing and sprinkle with the orange rind. Leave to set.

222 CHORNS

Preparation time:	YOU WILL NEED:
20 minutes	*75 g/3 oz plain flour*
	100 g/4 oz caster sugar
Cooking time:	*50 g/2 oz desiccated coconut*
12-15 minutes	*50 g/2 oz rolled oats*
	25 g/1 oz walnuts, chopped
Oven temperature:	*1 teaspoon bicarbonate of soda*
180C/350F/gas 4	*2 tablespoons golden syrup*
	100 g/4 oz butter
Makes about 25	*3 tablespoons water*
Calories:	
98 per portion	

Mix together the flour, sugar, coconut, oats, walnuts and bicarbonate of soda in a bowl. Put the syrup and butter in a saucepan. Heat gently until the butter has melted. Add the dry ingredients and the water to the saucepan and mix well.

Shape the mixture into balls about 2.5 cm/1 inch across. Place on greased baking trays, allowing space for the mixture to spread.

Bake for 12-15 minutes until golden brown. Leave on the baking tray for 2 minutes, then transfer to a wire rack to cool completely.

▨ COOK'S TIP

Any leftover centres of the rings that cannot be re-rolled to make more biscuits can be baked separately as small biscuits for children.

▨ COOK'S TIP

It is easier to shape sticky biscuit mixture into balls if you dampen your hands with cold water before beginning to shape the mixture.

Crunchies

223 WHOLEFOOD CRUNCHIES

Preparation time:	YOU WILL NEED:
20 minutes	50 g/2 oz plain flour
	1 teaspoon bicarbonate of soda
Cooking time:	75 g/3 oz wholemeal flour
about 45 minutes	125 g/4½ oz rolled oats
	250 g/9 oz light soft brown sugar
Oven temperature:	1 teaspoon lemon essence
190C/375F/gas 5	175 g/6 oz butter, melted
	FOR THE FILLING
Makes about 20	100 g/4 oz dried figs, chopped
	100 g/4 oz dried apricots, chopped
Calories:	1 teaspoon lemon essence
195 per portion	grated rind of 1 lemon
	200 ml/7 fl oz water
	FOR THE TOPPING
	1 tablespoon rolled oats
	2 tablespoons demerara sugar

Grease and line a shallow 28 x 18 cm/11 x 7 inch tin.

For the filling, put the figs and apricots into a saucepan with the essence, lemon rind and water. Bring to the boil and simmer 15 minutes. Remove the lid, stir and continue cooking until the mixture becomes thick but not dry. Leave to cool.

Sift the plain flour and bicarbonate of soda, then mix in the wholemeal flour, oats and sugar. Mix in the essence and butter.

Press half the mixture into the tin. Cover with the fruit mixture. Add the remaining oat mixture to cover the filling. Press down and sprinkle with a mixture of oats and demerara sugar for the topping. Bake for about 30 minutes or until lightly browned. Cool in the tin before cutting into squares.

▨ COOK'S TIP

To make banana crunchies, substitute 100 g/4 oz dried bananas, chopped, for the apricots in the filling. Use vanilla essence instead of the lemon in both the biscuits and the filling. Omit the grated lemon rind from the filling.

224 BARNSTAPLE GINGERBREADS

Preparation time:	YOU WILL NEED:
15 minutes, plus	50 g/2 oz butter
cooling	50 g/2 oz caster sugar
	75 g/3 oz golden syrup
Cooking time:	1 teaspoon lemon juice
10-12 minutes per	50 g/2 oz plain flour
batch	1 teaspoon ground ginger
Oven temperature:	
180C/350F/gas 4	
Makes 18-20	
Calories:	
61-55 per portion	

Put the butter, sugar and syrup in a saucepan. Heat gently until the butter has melted and the sugar has dissolved. Remove from the heat and add the lemon juice, flour and ginger. Mix well, then leave until cold.

Grease three baking trays. Place barely level teaspoons of the mixture with plenty of space between, on the baking trays. Bake one tray at a time for 10-12 minutes each.

When the biscuits are flat and golden brown, remove from the oven and cool for 1 minute. Remove with a palette knife and cool on a wire rack. Cook the remaining biscuits in the same way.

▨ COOK'S TIP

These biscuits are similar to brandy snaps but they are made flat instead of being rolled up. They are very good served with ice cream on a hot summer afternoon.

225 NUT CHOC CHIP BISCUITS

Preparation time:	YOU WILL NEED:
20 minutes, plus	*225 g/8 oz plain flour*
chilling	*1 teaspoon baking powder*
	100 g/4 oz margarine
Cooking time:	*150 g/5 oz caster sugar*
12-15 minutes	*25 g/1 oz toasted hazelnuts, finely*
	chopped
Oven temperature:	*25 g/1 oz plain or milk chocolate,*
190C/375F/gas 5	*finely chopped*
	1 tablespoon black treacle
Makes about 30	*3 tablespoons milk*

Calories:
about 86 per portion

Put the flour and baking powder in a bowl. Add the margarine, cut into pieces, and rub into the flour until the mixture resembles fine breadcrumbs. Stir in the sugar, nuts and chocolate. Add the treacle and milk and mix to a firm dough.

Turn out on to a floured surface and knead lightly. Shape into a roll 5 cm/2 inches thick and wrap in cling film. Chill for 30 minutes.

Cut the roll into thin slices and place a little apart on greased baking trays. Bake for 12-15 minutes until beginning to colour.

Remove from the oven and leave the biscuits for 1 minute, then transfer to a wire rack to cool. Store in an airtight tin.

226 PITCAITHLY BANNOCK

Preparation time:	YOU WILL NEED:
20 minutes	*150 g/5 oz plain flour*
	25 g/1 oz ground rice
Cooking time:	*100 g/4 oz butter, cut into pieces*
35 minutes	*75 g/3 oz caster sugar*
	25 g/1 oz chopped mixed peel
Oven temperature:	*25 g/1 oz unblanched almonds,*
160C/325F/gas 3	*finely chopped*
	1 tablespoon milk
Makes 16	*caster sugar, to sprinkle*

Calories:
127 per portion

Put the flour and ground rice in a bowl. Add the butter and rub in with the fingertips until the mixture resembles fine breadcrumbs. Stir in the sugar, peel and almonds. Add the milk and work with the hands until the mixture clings together. Divide the mixture in half.

Knead one piece of dough lightly until smooth. Place inside an 18 cm/7 inch fluted flan ring on a baking tray and press out evenly. Remove the ring carefully and repeat with the remaining dough. Prick both rounds all over with a fork.

Bake for 35 minutes until lightly coloured. Leave for 5 minutes, then sprinkle with caster sugar and cut each round into 8 triangles. Cool on a wire rack.

■ COOK'S TIP

To skin hazelnuts, place them on a baking tray under a preheated grill until the skins split, turning them frequently to prevent them burning. Then put the nuts in a plastic bag and rub them against each other.

■ COOK'S TIP

If you do not have a fluted flan ring, use a plain one and pinch the edge between a finger and thumb to decorate.

227 PEANUT BUTTER BISCUITS

Preparation time:
25 minutes

Cooking time:
12-15 minutes

Oven temperature:
200C/400F/gas 6

Makes about 50

Calories:
about 72 per portion

YOU WILL NEED:
275 g/10 oz plain flour
½ teaspoon baking powder
½ teaspoon salt
½ teaspoon bicarbonate of soda
100 g/4 oz margarine
225 g/8 oz soft light brown sugar
100 g/4 oz crunchy peanut butter
2 eggs, beaten

Sift the flour, baking powder, salt and bicarbonate of soda into a bowl. Add the margarine, cut into pieces, and rub into the flour until the mixture resembles fine breadcrumbs. Stir in the sugar. Add the peanut butter and beaten eggs and mix to a soft dough.

Form the dough into small balls, about 2.5 cm/1 inch across and place a little apart on greased baking trays. Mark each biscuit by pressing the surface with a fork to make a criss-cross pattern.

Bake for 12-15 minutes until risen. Remove and leave for 1 minute, then transfer to a wire rack to cool. Store the biscuits in an airtight tin.

228 SWEET BISCUIT DOUGH

Preparation time:
20 minutes, plus chilling

Cooking time:
about 10 minutes

Oven temperature:
180C/350F/gas 4

Makes 24-36
according to size

Calories:
96-64 per portion

YOU WILL NEED:
125 g/4½ oz butter
2-3 teaspoons grated lemon rind
    or ¼ teaspoon vanilla essence
100 g/4 oz caster sugar
2 egg yolks
225 g/8 oz plain flour, sifted

Cream the butter with the sugar and lemon rind or vanilla essence. Gradually beat in the egg yolks, then the flour and knead lightly. Chill for 30 minutes or until stiff.

Roll out the dough thinly on a floured board, using a floured rolling pin. Brush off any flour on top of the dough and cut into rounds, using a 5 cm/2 inch cutter. Alternatively, cut into rounds, then, using the same cutter, in half so you have a crescent and an oval shape. Separate the shapes and chill the biscuits until stiff.

Place on a greased baking tray and bake for about 10 minutes or until set and golden. Cool on a wire rack. Serve plain or decorated to taste.

■ COOK'S TIP

Use a butter or block margarine for baking biscuits. Soft tub margarine is not suitable as this is aerated which affects the quantity required.

■ COOK'S TIP

You can also cut larger rounds using a 7.5 cm/3 inch cutter. Stamp out the centres with a 2.5 cm/1 inch cuter. Separate the rings. Either knead the centres together lightly and roll out to make more rings, or bake as rounds, then sandwich together in pairs with jam.

CHEESECAKES

There are cheesecakes to suit all tastes here. Some are rich and crumbly, others smooth and creamy; some need baking, others need only to be chilled until required. Try giving basic, or favourite, cheesecakes variety by using different toppings and decorations or substituting a different kind of base. You will find various bases and toppings among the recipes here.

229 CRUNCHY CHEESECAKE TART

Preparation time:	YOU WILL NEED:
20 minutes	50 g/2 oz butter or margarine, melted
Cooking time:	100 g/4 oz shortcake biscuits, crushed
30-35 minutes	15 g/½ oz chopped walnuts
Oven temperature:	FOR THE FILLING
190C/375F/gas 5	225 g/8oz full fat soft cheese, softened
Serves 6	50 g/2 oz caster sugar
	2 eggs, beaten
Calories:	grated rind and juice of 1 lemon
426 per portion	225 g/8 oz fresh fruits, to decorate

In a bowl, mix together the melted butter and margarine, biscuit crumbs and chopped walnuts. Press the mixture over the base and sides of a 20 cm/8 inch ovenproof pie plate or flan dish.

To make the filling, place the cheese, sugar, beaten eggs, lemon rind and juice in a bowl. Whisk until smooth, preferably with an electric whisk.

Pour the mixture into the biscuit base and bake in a preheated oven for 30-35 minutes, until the filling is just set. Leave to cool.

Decorate the top of the cheesecake with circles of a selection of fresh fruit.

230 CONTINENTAL CHEESECAKE

Preparation time:	YOU WILL NEED:
25 minutes, plus	100 g/4 oz plain flour
chilling	pinch of salt
	50 g/2 oz margarine or butter, diced
Cooking time:	15 g/½ oz caster sugar
about 45 minutes	1 tablespoon cold water
	FOR THE FILLING
Oven temperature:	75 g/3 oz butter
180C/350F/gas 4	75 g/3 oz caster sugar
	2 eggs, lightly beaten
Serves 8	225 g/8 oz curd cheese, softened
	grated rind of 1 lemon
Calories:	2 tablespoons lemon juice
329 per portion	25 g/1 oz ground almonds

Grease a 23 cm/9 inch flan ring on a baking sheet.

Sift the flour with the salt into a bowl. Add the margarine and rub it in until the mixture resembles fine breadcrumbs. Stir in the sugar. Sprinkle over the water and draw the mixture together to make a firm dough, adding a little more water if necessary, to bind. Turn the dough on to a floured surface and knead for 1 minute, until smooth. Roll out and use to line the flan ring. Chill in the refrigerator for 20 minutes, then trim.

Cream the butter and sugar in a bowl until light and fluffy, then gradually beat in the eggs, alternating with the cheese. When thoroughly blended, stir in the lemon rind and juice and the ground almonds, mixing well. Pour the filling into the prepared flan ring and bake in a preheated oven for 45 minutes, or until set.

■ COOK'S TIP

Fruits which would taste well on top of this cheesecake include strawberries, grapes, satsuma segments and sliced bananas or kiwi fruit.

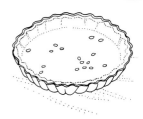

■ COOK'S TIP

Scatter 25 g/1 oz seedless raisins over the base of the pastry case before pouring in the filling.

231 POLISH CHEESECAKES

Preparation time:
about 40 minutes,
plus chilling

Cooking time:
50-60 minutes

Oven temperature:
180C/350F/gas 4

Makes 12

Calories:
408 per portion

YOU WILL NEED:
pâte sucrée (see Cook's Tip)
FOR THE FILLING
225 g/8 oz full fat soft cheese
4 egg yolks
50 g/2 oz butter, melted
225 g/8 oz caster sugar
grated rind of ½ lemon or orange
a few drops of vanilla essence
FOR THE TOPPING
100 g/4 oz icing sugar, sifted
2-3 tablespoons strained lemon or
  orange juice
glacé fruits

Make the pâte sucrée, wrap in polythene and chill for 1 hour.

Roll out the pastry and use to line a lightly greased tin about 28 x 18 x 4 cm/11 x 7 x 1½ inches. Beat the cheese until smooth and then beat in the egg yolks, butter, sugar, fruit, rind and essence. Put the mixture into the pastry case and level out evenly. Bake in a preheated oven for about 50-60 minutes or until quite firm. Leave to cool in the tin.

Use the icing sugar and fruit juice to make a fairly thin glacé icing and spread a thin layer over the cheesecake. When beginning to set mark into fingers or squares and decorate each with pieces or slices of glacé fruits. When cold cut into fingers or squares.

232 AMERICAN CHEESECAKE

Preparation time:
15 minutes

Cooking time:
about 45 minutes

Oven temperature:
180C/350F/gas 4

Serves 10-12

Calories:
745-621 per portion

YOU WILL NEED:
75 g/3 oz margarine or butter,
  melted
175 g/6 oz digestive biscuits,
  crushed
FOR THE FILLING
1 kg/2 lb full fat soft cheese
250 g/9 oz caster sugar
4 eggs, lightly beaten
40 g/1½ oz plain flour, sifted
300 ml/½ pint soured cream
grated rind of 1 lemon
fresh or drained canned cherries,
  to decorate

Grease a loose-bottomed or spring-form 23 cm/9 inch cake tin. Mix the melted margarine with the biscuit crumbs. Spoon into the greased tin and press evenly over the base. Place on a baking sheet and bake in a preheated oven for 10 minutes, then set aside to cool.

Beat together all the ingredients for the filling except the cherries and pour into the tin on the baking sheet. Bake in the oven for 35 minutes, or until set. Leave for 3-4 hours, until cold.

Run a round-bladed knife around the sides of the cheesecake, then remove from the tin. Transfer to a serving plate and decorate with cherries.

COOK'S TIP

Pâte sucrée: sift on to a work surface 150 g/6 oz plain flour and a pinch of salt. Make a well in the centre, add 75 g/3 oz sugar, 75 g/3oz butter and 3 egg yolks and work together with the fingertips, gradually pulling in the flour to give a smooth, pliable dough.

COOK'S TIP

While the cherries are a typically American fruit for this cheesecake, you could use other berry fruits, such as redcurrants, raspberries or strawberries.

233 RAISIN CHEESECAKE

Preparation time:
about 25 minutes,
plus cooling

Cooking time:
1 hour

Oven temperature:
180C/350F/gas 4

Makes 1 x 23 cm/9
inch cheesecake

Total calories:
3016

YOU WILL NEED:
100 g/4 oz shortcrust pastry
300 g/12 oz cream cheese
2 large eggs, separated
100 g/4 oz caster sugar
4 tablespoons milk
50 g/2 oz plain flour
½ teaspoon vanilla essence
1 teaspoon finely grated lemon rind
50 g/2 oz stoned or seedless raisins

Well grease a 23 cm/9 inch loose-bottomed cake tin or spring-form pan. Roll the pastry out thinly, cut into a 2 cm/9 inch circle and place in the bottom of the tin.

Beat the cream cheese, then beat in the egg yolks, sugar, milk, flour, vanilla essence, lemon rind and raisins. Mix well. Whisk the egg whites until they form stiff peaks, then fold into the cheese mixture. Turn into the tin on top of the pastry.

Bake in a moderate oven for 1 hour or until the cheesecake is set. Turn off the oven and leave the cake inside to cool, for about 2 hours; this helps to prevent it from sinking in the centre. Remove from the tin before serving.

■ COOK'S TIP

Use vanilla essence, made from the vanilla bean pod, rather than vanilla flavouring, as the flavour is much better.

234 HEAVENLY CHEESECAKE

Preparation time:
25 minutes

Cooking time:
1½-1¾ hours

Oven temperature:
160C/325F/gas 3

Serves 8

Calories:
552 per portion

YOU WILL NEED:
50 g/2 oz self-raising flour
½ teaspoon baking powder
50 g/2 oz butter, softened
50 g/2 oz caster sugar
1 egg
a few drops cochineal
FOR THE FILLING
300 g/11 oz full fat soft cheese
40 g/1½ oz plain flour, sifted
150 ml/5 fl oz whipping cream
a few drops of vanilla essence
5 egg whites
100 g/4 oz caster sugar
FOR THE ICING
225 g/8 oz icing sugar
1 egg white, lightly whisked
crystallized rose petals

Grease a loose-bottomed 18-20 cm/7-8 inch cake tin. Sift the flour and baking powder into a bowl. Add the margarine, sugar, egg and cochineal. Beat until blended. Spread the mixture evenly over the base of the tin.

Make the filling: beat the cheese until softened. Beat in the flour, cream, essence, 1 egg white and half the sugar. Fold into the cheese mixture and turn into the tin. Bake for 1½-1¾ hours or until set. Cool for 1 hour, remove from the tin on to a plate.

For the icing, sift the sugar into a bowl and beat in the egg white. Swirl the icing over the cake and leave until just setting, then scatter over the rose petals. Chill for 2-3 hours.

■ COOK'S TIP

To crystallize rose petals, brush with egg white, sift over caster sugar and leave to dry.

235 DEVIL'S FOOD CHEESECAKE

Preparation time:	YOU WILL NEED:
25 minutes	75 g/3 oz butter, melted
	25 g/1 oz caster sugar
Cooking time:	175 g/6 oz chocolate digestive
1¾-2 hours	biscuits, crushed
	FOR THE FILLING
Oven temperature:	100 g/4 oz plain dessert chocolate
160C/325F/gas 3	300 g/10 oz full fat soft cheese
	3 eggs, separated
Serves 8	1 teaspoon gravy browning
	50 g/2 oz soft dark brown sugar
Calories:	25 g/1 oz plain flour, sifted
852 per portion	150 ml/¼ pint soured cream
	50 g/3 oz caster sugar
	chocolate frosting (see Cook's Tip)

Grease a loose-bottomed or spring-form 18-20 cm/7-8 inch tin. Mix the butter with the sugar and biscuit crumbs. Spoon into the tin and press over the base. Chill while making the filling.

Break the chocolate into pieces and put in a heatproof bowl set over a saucepan of hot water. Heat gently, until melted.

Beat the cheese in a bowl until softened. Beat in the egg yolks, gravy browning, sugar, flour, soured cream and melted chocolate. Whisk the egg whites until stiff, then whisk in the caster sugar. Fold into the cheese mixture. Turn into the prepared tin and smooth the surface. Place the cheesecake on a baking sheet and bake in a preheated oven for 1½-1¾ hours or until set. Cool for 1 hour, then remove from the tin to a wire rack. Make the frosting and swirl it over the top and sides of the cheesecake. Transfer to a plate and chill for 2-3 hours.

■ COOK'S TIP

For the frosting, gently dissolve 225 g/8 oz sugar in 150 ml/¼ pint water over a low heat. Bring to the boil and boil gently until syrupy. Beat in 175 g/6 oz broken up plain chocolate. When chocolate has melted, add 50 g/2 oz margarine and beat until thick and glossy.

236 PINEAPPLE WHOLEFOOD CHEESECAKE

Preparation time:	YOU WILL NEED:
20 minutes	75 g/3 oz margarine or butter,
	melted
Cooking time:	1 teaspoon ground cinnamon
30 minutes	1 teaspoon soft dark brown sugar
	175 g/6 oz wholemeal bran
Oven temperature:	biscuits, crushed
180C/350F/gas 4	FOR THE FILLING
	225 g/8 oz curd cheese
Serves 6	3 tablespoons clear honey
	150 ml/¼ pint soured cream
Calories:	1 egg yolk
440 per portion	1 small ripe fresh pineapple,
	peeled, cored and chopped
	1-2 tablespoons sesame seeds

Grease a loose-bottomed or spring-form 20-23 cm/8-9 inch cake tin. Mix the melted margarine with the cinnamon, sugar and biscuit crumbs. Spoon into the greased tin and press evenly over the base. Chill while making the filling.

Put the cheese, honey, soured cream and egg yolk into a bowl and beat until evenly blended. Pour the mixture into the tin. Place the cheesecake on a baking sheet. Bake in the oven for 30 minutes, or until just set. Leave the cheesecake for 3-4 hours, until cold.

Remove the cheesecake from the tin and transfer to a serving plate. Arrange the pineapple in a ring around the top of the cheesecake. Sprinkle the sesame seeds in the centre.

■ COOK'S TIP

Other fresh fruit such as hulled strawberries, raspberries, sliced kiwi fruit or halved and seeded grapes, can be used instead of pineapple. For extra interest, decorate the cheesecake with sprigs of mint or lemon balm.

237 APRICOT CHEESECAKE

Preparation time: 25 minutes	YOU WILL NEED: 75 g/3 oz butter, melted 50 g/2 oz soft light brown sugar
Cooking time: 1½-1¾ hours	100 g/4 oz porridge oats 1 egg yolk FOR THE FILLING
Oven temperature: 160C/325F/gas 3	2 x 425 g/15 oz cans apricot halves, drained 225 g/8 oz curd cheese
Serves 8	3 eggs, separated a few drops almond essence
Calories: 462 per portion	100 g/4 oz caster sugar 25 g/1 oz plain flour, sifted 300 ml/½ pint whipping cream

Grease a loose-bottomed or spring-form 18-20 cm/7-8 inch tin. Mix the butter with the sugar, oats and egg yolk. Spoon into the tin and press over base. Reserve 8 apricot halves for decoration, chop the remainder and scatter over the oat base.

Beat the cheese in a bowl. Beat in the egg yolks, almond essence, half the sugar, the flour and half the cream. Whisk the egg whites until stiff, then whisk in the remaining sugar. Using a large metal spoon, fold lightly, but thoroughly, into the cheese mixture. Turn into the tin and smooth the surface.

Place the cheesecake on a baking sheet and bake in a preheated oven for 1½-1¾ hours, or until the filling is set. Leave the cheesecake for 3-4 hours, until cold, then remove from the tin. Transfer to a plate.

Whip the remaining cream and pipe in swirls round the edge of the cake. Slice the reserved apricots and put on top.

■ COOK'S TIP

Try canned peaches instead of apricots in this cheesecake.

238 SPICED PEAR CHEESECAKE

Preparation time: 25 minutes	YOU WILL NEED: 75 g/3 oz butter, melted 50 g/2 oz caster sugar
Cooking time: 1½-1¾ hours	pinch of ground mixed spice 175 g/6 oz digestive biscuits, crushed
Oven temperature: 160C/325F/gas 3	FOR THE FILLING 225 g/8 oz curd cheese
Serves 8	3 eggs, separated ½ teaspoon ground mixed spice 100 g/4 oz caster sugar
Calories: 511 per portion	grated rind of ½ lemon 1 tablespoon lemon juice 2 pears, peeled, cored, chopped 40 g/1½ oz plain flour, sifted 75 g/3 oz Cheddar cheese, grated 6 tablespoons soured cream

Grease a loose-bottomed 18-20 cm/7-8 inch tin. Mix the butter with the sugar, spice and biscuit crumbs. Spoon into the tin and press evenly over the base. Chill while making the filling.

Beat the cheese into a bowl. Beat in the egg yolks, spice, 50 g/2 oz sugar, lemon rind and juice, chopped pears, flour, grated cheese and soured cream. Whisk the egg whites until stiff, then whisk in the remaining sugar. Fold lightly, but thoroughly, into the cheese mixture. Turn into the tin and smooth the surface.

Place the cheesecake on a baking sheet and bake in a preheated oven for 1½-1¾ hours, or until the filling is set. Let the cheesecake cool for 1 hour, then transfer to a plate and decorate (see Cook's Tip). Chill for 2-3 hours before serving.

■ COOK'S TIP

Decorate the cheesecake with 4 sliced canned pear halves, some chopped angelica and piped double cream (about 150 ml/¼ pint).

239 DELUXE GINGER CHEESECAKE

Preparation time:	YOU WILL NEED:
25 minutes	75 g/3 oz butter, melted
	50 g/2 oz caster sugar
Cooking time:	175 g/6 oz gingernuts, crushed
1½-1¾ hours	FOR THE FILLING
	300 g/10 oz curd cheese
Oven temperature:	3 eggs, separated
160C/325F/gas 3	3 tablespoons black treacle, warmed
	50 g/2 oz soft light brown sugar
Serves 8	grated rind of ½ lemon
	1 tablespoon lemon juice
Calories:	25 g/1 oz plain flour, sifted
479 per portion	2 teaspoons ground ginger
	6 tablespoons soured cream
	50 g/2 oz caster sugar
	75 g/3 oz crystallized ginger, chopped
	150 ml/¼ pint double or whipping cream, lightly whipped

Grease a loose-bottomed or spring-form 18-20 cm/7-8 inch cake tin. Mix the butter with the sugar and biscuit crumbs. Spoon into the tin and press evenly over the base. Chill.

Beat the cheese in a bowl until softened. Beat in the egg yolks, treacle, brown sugar, lemon rind and juice, flour, ginger and soured cream. Whisk the egg whites till stiff, then whisk in the caster sugar. Fold thoroughly into the cheese mixture, with the ginger. Turn into the tin. Place the cheesecake on a baking sheet and bake for 1½-1¾ hours, or until set. Cool for 1 hour. Pipe the cream over the top. Chill for 2-3 hours before serving.

▥ COOK'S TIP

To crush the ginger biscuits, put between 2 sheets of greaseproof paper or in a plastic bag and crush with a rolling pin. To carry the ginger flavour into the decoration, scatter chopped stem ginger over the top.

240 FUN-TIME CHEESECAKE

Preparation time:	YOU WILL NEED:
25 minutes	50 g/2 oz butter, melted
	50 g/2 oz caster sugar
Cooking time:	100 g/4 oz digestive biscuits, crushed
3-4 minutes	FOR THE FILLING
Serves 8-10	1 x 15 g/½ oz sachet powdered gelatine
Calories:	3 tablespoons water
249-199 per portion	225 g/8 oz cottage cheese, sieved
	2 eggs, separated
	100 g/4 oz caster sugar
	grated rind of ½ lemon
	a few drops of vanilla essence
	150 g/6 oz fruit yogurt
	assorted small sweets, to decorate

Grease a loose-bottomed or spring-form 18-20 cm/7-8 inch cake tin. Make the biscuit base as in recipe 238. Chill. Sprinkle the gelatine over the water in a heatproof bowl and leave for 2-3 minutes until spongy. Stand the bowl in a pan of hot water and stir until the gelatine has dissolved. Set aside to cool slightly.

Place the cheese in a bowl and beat in the egg yolks, half the sugar, lemon rind, vanilla essence and yogurt. Stir in the liquid gelatine. Leave the mixture until on the point of setting. Whisk the egg whites until stiff, then whisk in the remaining sugar. Fold thoroughly, into the cheese mixture. Turn the mixture into the prepared tin and gently tip and tilt it to level the surface. Chill for 3-4 hours, or until set. Transfer the cheesecake to a plate. Decorate with sweets.

▥ COOK'S TIP

Use free-range eggs. Do not serve this cheesecake, with its uncooked eggs, to very small children, elderly people, or pregnant women.

INDEX